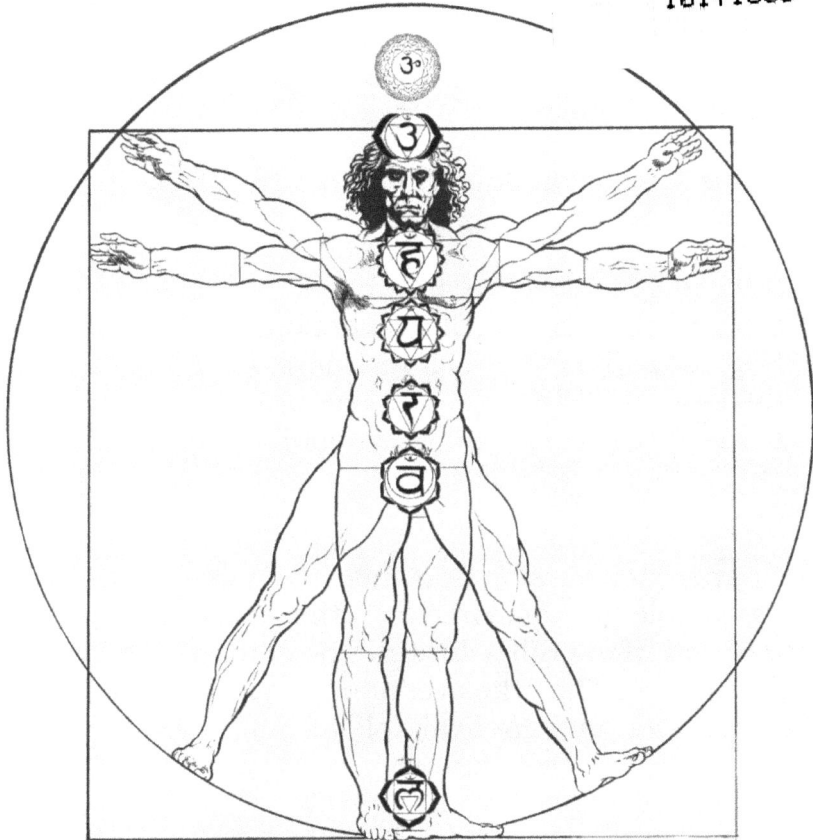

Jesus on Elevated Form.

Lars Gimstedt

Edition 1, revision date June 1 2015.

ISBN
978-91-88137-15-9   (Paper back)
978-91-88137-16-6   (EPUB version)
978-91-88137-17-3   (LIT version)
978-91-88137-18-0   (MOBI version)
978-91-88137-19-7   (PDF version)

The paperback version and the Kindle version (MOBI) are available on Amazon.com, other Amazon internet stores and many other internet bookshops affiliated with Amazon. The other versions, including the Swedish versions, are available at
http://psykosyntesforum.se/
Jesus_on_Elevated_Form.htm

Typeface Bookman Old 12. Page size 6x9" (15,24x22,86 cm) Margins: hor 2,0, vert 2,0.

About the author:

Lars Gimstedt works as a psychotherapist in Linkoping, Sweden. His formal training was as a quantum physicist, and he has worked as an engineer and a manager in corporate business for 30 years.

In the middle of his life, he started to study Psychosynthesis, CBT and NLP, and worked part time as a psychotherapist during ten years, until he started to work full time in his company PsychosynthesisForum.com in 2003 with life and leadership coaching, psychotherapy and with internet e-courses and e-books.

Previous books by Lars Gimstedt:

Stairway. 10 Steps to heaven. (March 2014)
I, Yeshua. Awakener. (May 2014)
A Course *To* Miracles. (Edited by Lars G, Nov 2014)
Jesus on Catching the Bull. (March 2015)

Index

Prologue.

Hi again, Jesus.

Hi, Lars! You're on it again, aren't you? Another book, already!

It was such fun writing the last one, our exploration on Catching the Bull. And, I have been longing for you, to talk like this again.

And I have been longing for you. I hope you don't mind my nudging at your thoughts like this, making you "get the idea" of starting our dialogue again.

I don't mind, because I have become aware that you do. I know you have done it always, but I was just not aware of it before. Now I am, and I even want you to. It's even so that I don't really differentiate between "your" thoughts and "mine" any longer.

But, that you can do this with everybody simultaneously, that still boggles my mind...

Good thing I made you in <u>my</u> likeness, and not the opposite, because then I would be like the image of God in the cartoon you found on the internet a while ago:

"Sorry, I can't—I have to be everywhere."

Yes, as soon as we try to put you into form, we make up images like this one. But you must have experienced this, though, whilst living on Earth?

Yes I have, very much so. The scriptures about my life describe a number of times when both I and my disciples were weary of exhaustion, when people wanted us to "be everywhere". Being outside of time has its pros and cons, and being able to be everywhere is a definite pro.

Funny, I haven't thought of this before as something having pros and cons. Does being outside of time really have any cons?

Not many, I agree, and when we all have returned Home there will be none. But till then, one con is not meeting in form. Being able to see and be seen with the eyes of the body, to touch, to hear the voice, all these give extra dimensions to communicating.

Do you miss it?

No, I don't need to miss it. You forget all the ones having become fully aware of their Christ consciousness - I share their experiences all the time, and I enjoy all of it tremendously. I am with you on Earth in more ways than you know.

But in these cases you want to be "hidden", and not as in the open and as outspoken as you were as the man Jesus?

There are many different ways in which my Plan for the Atonement and the Awakening is unfolding. In order to be effective, some ways need to be covert; others (like this one) need to be more overt. Many are something in between, where some can choose to see me behind what's happening, others don't need to and can choose to see it as made up by a person's mind.

I don't want the Atonement to be forced upon anyone. It is effective only if it comes out of one's honest willingness and choice. It is important that for example this text can be interpreted both as inspired by me, or as a result of your creative mind only.

I have to admit that I vacillate between both of these interpretations myself, all the time...

Your willingness to stay open for the <u>possibility</u> of more than one interpretation is all that is needed.

When I hear you say that you are here with me just now in the open, I again feel how my ego boosts itself. I do not any longer identify with its thoughts, but I feel how they still influence me...

Being aware of them is good enough, you will be OK.

And, when I once said "if two of you on earth agree about anything they ask for, it will be done for them by my Father in heaven." What I could not explain then was how this statement really should be for those that have awakened to their true Selves.

For these, and in this group of people I am <u>one</u> of the members, the statement should be "if two of us agree about anything, it is already done".

So, to put this into its proper perspective: encounters like ours here are going on in many other places, many more than I think you can dream of!

And when you ultimately will become able to wholeheartedly agree with me on something, this <u>will</u> become the New Reality for you.

That <u>would</u> be a happy dream... Is this New Reality the same thing that you called The Happy Dream in A Course in Miracles?

Yes, it is. It is unfolding, and much time will be saved for mankind.

But much unnecessary time will still be wasted, and much unnecessary suffering will still plague you, as the collective ego fights back viciously in many places.

What should we do about this? Personally, I weep inside reading about what's happening in many other countries, seeing it on TV, and I feel powerless and frustrated. This collective ego-poison is creeping in over the borders of even my peaceful country as well, in many forms.

Firstly, you need to stop them from hurting others and thereby themselves, if needed also with appropriate force. Be aware though not to promote martyrdom, as this just reinforces ego thoughts.

Secondly, you need to reach out to them in many different ways with Forgiveness and Love. I ask you sincerely, as I asked My Father, "Forgive them, for they know not what they are doing."

But the ones that try to stop them with ego-reactions of the same kind, just meeting violence with violence, and by that just "creating more terrorism"? What can be done with these people, groups and governments?

There is but <u>one</u> answer to all that happens, whether it comes out of love or out of fear, and the answer is Love. Forgive these ones as well, they don't really know what they are doing either, and continue to reach out with Right-mindedness, Forgiveness and Love. Sanity <u>will</u> return, even if many things just now seem to show the opposite.

I wish I had your confidence... but again, you surely have "inside information" helping you to be confident.

I don't, you have access to everything I know. But as long as you believe that you don't, it will be as you believe. I invite you to be confident "without cause". If you so want, you can <u>choose</u> to trust me. Choose again!

OK, OK, I know... But, you're right. I, and we all, need to be reminded. Thank you for doing it. And please, keep doing it. But, I don't need to ask you to, do I - you <u>have</u> been reminding us from the beginning of time, haven't you?

I know you know this in your heart, and it pleases me that you know.

But, now, what more is it you want to talk with me about? You have started to let this dialogue unfold here, in the prologue of something you up to now have just called "Next book".

Truly, I don't know! I wish inspiration could just flow into me.

A good wish to start with. The word "Inspire" comes from the Latin expression "In Spiritus", which mean "in the Spirit". Your Webster dictionary gives several interpretations of the word Inspiration, but the first one is actually "a divine influence or action on a person believed to qualify him or her to receive and communicate sacred revelation".

I really have to watch my ego - now it swells up again in self-inflation... At the same time as it criticizes - "Who do you think you are, allowing yourself to write down things like that?" I really feel torn...

But, OK, if I would allow myself to believe "ask and you will be given", what do you give me?

I choose to interpret your request as "how can I open myself up to receiving inspiration?"

I propose the method called Structured Meditation. I know you already know it, so I will describe it here for the benefit of our readers:

First, "The Emptying Phase":
Take sheets of paper and divide them into two columns. Above the left one, write "My next book". Above the right column, write "Unrelated". Spend time, which can be days or weeks, writing down every thought, idea, or association you can come up with regarding "My next book", in the leftmost column.

Whenever thoughts or ideas come up that you feel are _not_ related to your next book, write these down into the _right_ column. Continue with this phase until the whole issue feels completely exhausted, and you cannot any longer come up with anything more at all, even if you try to force yourself to do it.

Secondly, "_The Reduction Phase_":
Cut away the rightmost columns from your sheets of paper, and throw them away. Spend time, which again can be days or weeks, crossing out with a pencil any statement that intuitively feels _less_ important than the others, even if it may feel important in itself. Continue doing this until you have _ten_ items left on your list. Towards the end of this phase this may feel difficult, so take your time in selecting which ones to cross out.

Thirdly and finally, the "_Receiving Phase_":
Write down the ten thoughts or ideas left on your long list on a new sheet of paper, with large letters. Use colored pencils if you want to make them stand out clearer. Spend time each day, somewhere between half an hour to several hours, meditating on this list. Try to listen to your Inner Silence. Continue doing this for days or weeks, until inspiration comes and you feel a strong urge to start working with your new book.

That's advice I use to give others now and then - I could have thought of that myself!

You just did. Or you didn't... Just kidding ;)
But, what about it?

OK, OK, I will do it.

....

....

Must be some sub-conscious lack of confidence in myself: I got surprised that advice I have given others works on myself!

I didn't have to do the Structured Meditation for long before I had an idea, one that made me feel an urge to go on with. I even got the title for the book at once: "Jesus on Elevated Form".

Congratulations! I assume that you with Elevated Form mean the notion I introduced in A Course of Love, the Elevated Self of Form?

Yes, I do. I loved the notion as soon as I first read about it. There is so much talk in A Course in Miracles (ACIM) about the illusory world we perceive, and about the Real World of God, and also about "The Happy Dream", the intermediate stage between these two worlds. But, in ACIM there is no real advice on how to reach The Happy Dream.

The editor of A Course of Love (ACOL) says in the foreword, describing one of the new concepts in ACOL as compared to ACIM:

> "It emphasizes 'being who you are' in a way that does not negate the personal self or the body. It reveals how the human form can be transformed into 'the Elevated Self of form', and how an illusory world will be made 'new' - divine - through relationship and unity."

As I see form as something we originally created, rather than something that has existed always, I have taken the freedom to change the term "Elevated Self of form" to "Elevated Self in form".

Am I correct in assuming that your term, which I here have abbreviated to Elevated Form, is a description of those who have come near "The Happy Dream"?

Yes, you are, if you emphasize "come near". They have not yet fully come into The Happy Dream, which is a more collective experience, but they have met the necessary conditions for it.

The title you have chosen - "Jesus on Elevated Form": I assume from this that you wish to include my input in a discussion around this notion, and that you wish to enter a dialogue, a new joint venture, about an exploration of the notion of Elevated Self in Form?

Yes, absolutely!

My previous book, "Jesus on Catching the Bull" was about a structured process for becoming aware of one's True Self. In my Structured Meditation, I felt that something is still missing for me, something I personally need to explore.

This is the "opposite" journey. If the Awakening is likened with <u>ascending</u> a mountain and finally reaching the top, the next journey <u>I</u> feel a need of exploring is the one where one <u>descends</u> back down to Earth again in order to manifest this new awareness there, in concrete action.

Even if I brought up the idea in ACOL of being on the mountain top <u>simultaneously</u> as being in the middle of one's ordinary life, I understand your need in this, and I would very much like to join with you in this exploration.

The more we talk about this, the more enthusiastic I feel!

No surprise - the word "enthusiasm" comes from Latin and Greek and means "divine inspiration"...

But, to continue: I feel that the notion Elevated Self in Form is connected to the notion "Self-actualization".

On the site of my company, PsychosynthesisForum.com, there is an interactive guide where one can explore where one is on one's Path towards Self-actualization, with ten different levels described. Each step in the guide includes questions with which one can assess how much one needs to work with the level in question. The levels are Self-esteem, Self-awareness, Self-assurance, Self-beliefs, Self-values, Self-image, Self-leadership, Self-mission, Self-vision and Self-actualization. The questions of the last one are:

"You will benefit from working with this level if

- You feel alone with your dreams, and it feels difficult to find a context that would support you.

- You often doubt yourself, despite the fact that you know what you want and where you want to go.

- You have visions, but it feels like you constantly need to revise them, due to unforeseeable things that happen in your life.

- You want to believe in a spiritual dimension, but as you never see any clear indications of that it exists, you often doubt that it does.

On the other hand, you are probably fairly ready with this level if

- You know you share your dreams with many, and seemingly by random they cross your path with the help you just then need.

- You burn for your Vision and your Mission, and you carry a conviction that you have what you need.   '

- You often have to re-prioritize and to change your actions plans, but only so that you again find the path that leads to your Vision.

- You often experience things that tell you that you are led by Someone that knows you and that has a plan for you and your life."

This is a good start! Knowing your "inner engineer", I assume you have come up with some kind of structure for working with "descending the mountain"?

Yes, you know me... Which feels nice, and practical - I don't need to explain myself a lot to you.

At the stage you still reside, I think it might feel good for you to know that even if I know you well, and even if I know about everything that has happened in your life, I cannot as yet share your thoughts. I cannot because you have not as yet become able to choose to share all what you are, as you do not yet know who you are in Truth.

But, don't feel taken down by this - you are on your way. And this exploration on which we now will embark will be an important step for you.

So, tell me about the structure you have decided to use!

In this exploration, I would like to use the ancient concept of Chakras, a model of the different centers of energy in our body, developed within Eastern religions, primarily Hinduism.

The most common way of working with one's Chakras is working from the bottom and up. This work is often aimed at "opening up" the Chakras in order to allow the "Kundalini Energy", the energy of Life, to flow freely upwards. In most traditions one starts with one's Root Chakra, situated at the bottom of the spine, and works upwards towards the Crown Chakra situated on the top of one's head.

What I envision us doing here though, is working in the opposite direction: the <u>final</u> stage described in "Jesus on Catching the Bull", Enlightenment, will be the <u>starting</u> point here.

My hope is that finding concrete ways of working with each Chakra <u>down</u>wards will "open up" for Divine Energy to flow down and <u>out</u> into concrete action in the world.

As for now, I have a very fuzzy picture of what to do, how to do it; and whether I will be able to find what I hope for: how to reach the state of Elevated Self in Form.

What's your input to this?

Wonderful! As you did in your former book, I like the idea of again using symbols and ideas from other religious traditions than the Christian ones. As I have said before, *"A universal theology is impossible, but a universal experience is not only possible but necessary."*

My first suggestion here is similar to what I suggested in your latest book: Just insert the symbols of the Chakras, together with an explanation of what each Chakra stands for and what common practices there are for opening it up, and we can then together explore how this can be used in the quest we have taken on: Describing a workable Path to the Elevated Self in Form.

Ah - even if, as I said, I haven't the foggiest on what will evolve here, I really burn for going into this!

It is a good thing that my mind, in doing this, is working outside of time, where your mind resides, because I now know from my experience of putting together "Jesus on Catching the Bull" that there will be many breaks in this work. Working outside of time gave me the somewhat spooky feeling that I was all the time being in constant dialogue, despite the breaks, even if they become long like days or weeks. I am confident that it will be the same now.

It will. It will also be as it was then, that your mind wanders away somewhere else, and you will leave The Now, and by that the unity with me. But as I have reminded you before: it doesn't matter - when you discover that you have floated away into the past or into the future, just gracefully return and we will continue where you left off.

I feel curious as well - even if I am well acquainted with the concept of chakras from my journeys in the East, I have never thought about how to use the concept together with the Atonement. I am looking forward to the exploration, beginning with the description of the uppermost Chakra, the Crown Chakra!

One word of caution though before we begin:

As I mentioned before, in your latest book, one should stay aware of that the "process" we now will be describing and exploring is not chronologically time-bound, where one is expected to follow the steps one after another. Rather, the different steps describe different levels of awareness and being, and in way they "happen" simultaneously. For different persons, there can be more and different things blocking one "Chakra level" than in the other ones, and each person may have to work with this structure in his or her individual way.

1. The Crown Chakra.

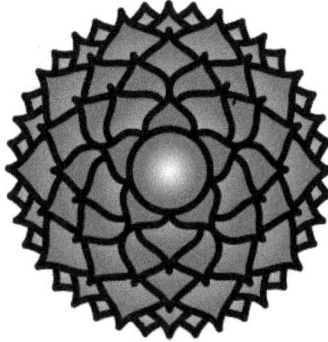

First, some general information about Chakras and the Chakra System.

The seven major energy centers described in this book (there are a number of minor ones as well) correspond to nerve ganglia located along the spine of the body (see the image below). The Chakra System can be seen as a chain that connects universal polarities: spirit-matter, heaven-earth, mind-body, a chain bringing these polarities into union. The word "Yoga", the tradition from which the Chakra System originates, actually means "Union".

When the Chakras are aligned and connected, two major currents of energy can flow freely - the current of liberation that flows upwards and the current of manifestation that flows downwards. This book will focus on the latter current of life energy.

The Chakras can also be likened to a row of lenses that condense thoughts into shape and form, transforming them first to inner images, then to words, actions and finally into material form.

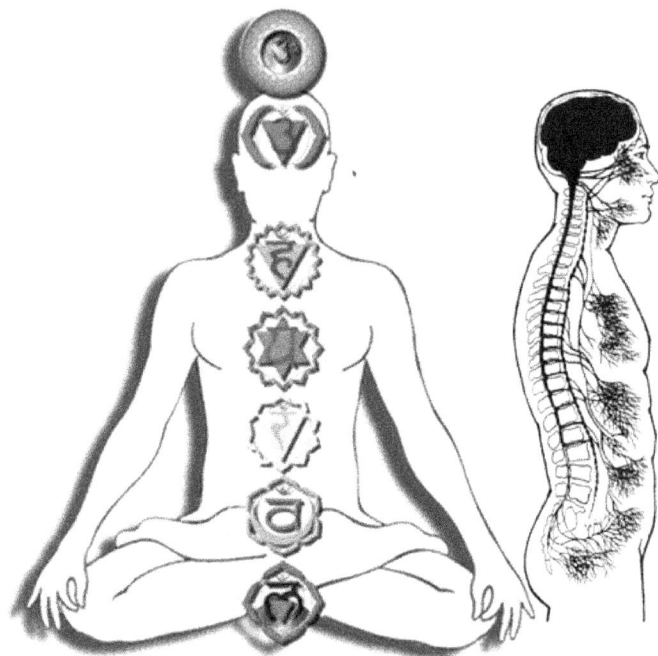

In the table below, a very brief description is presented in a table of the seven major Chakras. The table lists the <u>name</u> of the chakra, <u>the physical location</u> in the body, which <u>element</u> that is involved, the <u>color</u> commonly used for each chakra, and the psychological and spiritual <u>qualities</u> connected to each chakra.

The first four ones from the bottom have a special influence on personality traits. For you who are interested in exploring this, go to the internet page http://psykosyntesforum.se/elementity.htm, for assessing your personality profile in terms of the elements Earth, Water, Fire and Wind. This profile may indicate which of your chakras you express clearly, and which ones you may need to work with.

Name	Location	Element	Color	Qualities
Crown	Top of the head	Inform-ation	Violet	Awareness, Knowledge
Third Eye	Centre of forehead	Light	Indigo	Perception, Imagination
Throat	Base of throat	Sound	Blue	Communication, Creativity
Heart	Center of chest	Wind	Green	Compassion, Relationship
Solar Plexus	Solar Plexus	Fire	Yellow	Will, Spontaneity, Self-esteem
Sacral	Beneath the navel	Water	Orange	Feeling, Pleasure
Base	Peri-neum	Earth	Red	Trust, Stability, Grounding

The Crown Chakra, the uppermost one, situated at the crown of your head, is the entry point of Universal Spirit into your mind and body, an entry point which is needed as long as your mind and body are perceived as separated from the Divine.

It is symbolized by the ancient symbol "Sahasrara", a Sanskrit word that which means "The Thousand-petaled Lotus". The many petals stand for everything around you competing for your attention. In the middle of the lotus there is small white point, which symbolizes your centered, pure and silent awareness.

Staying centered helps you to keep connected with the Source of Divine Energy, without getting pulled away by events, people, voices, urges, thoughts and emotions.

The Crown Chakra's function is to transform the formless Divine Energy into personal consciousness, which is built up by images, beliefs, "thought-forms".

The most important tools for clearing out anything stopping the energy flow of manifestation on this level are meditation and contemplation. There are practices for this in many different forms. Which form one chooses to use depends on one's preferred focus of attention and which goal one has with one's spiritual practice, but the primary form of meditation should be to meditate on The Inner Silence.

On my website PsychosynthesisForum.com, there is a visualization that may be helpful in meditating on The Inner Silence, The Temple, where you are guided up on a mountain and into The Temple of Silence. (http://psykosyntesforum.se/ps_visualizations.htm.)

So, how is this as a first introduction of the Chakra System?

Very good, very informative! Neither too brief nor too extensive. I am sure you will have caught the interest of the one reading this just now, who probably now is curious on how to open up his or her own chakras.

But, and here I might sound as I am being critical: there is something one needs to be aware of, before going into this. You will see that this is not criticism of the Chakra System; rather it is about how to regard a concept like this all together.

The Chakra System is a <u>model</u> of how the body interacts with Divine Energy. As such, it belongs to the world of form, and can therefore be illusionary, as is everything in form if it is perceived as separate from the divine. This does not mean that The Chakra System is meaningless - it is a neutral thing in itself, as is the body with its thoughts and emotions. If the Chakra System is meaningful to utilize or not, depends on what it is used <u>for</u>. In A Course in Miracles I said, in the beginning:

> *"Child of God, you were created to create the good, the beautiful and the holy. Do not forget this. The Love of God, for a little while, must still be expressed through one body to another, because vision is still so dim. You can use your body best to help you enlarge your perception so you can achieve real vision, of which the physical eye is incapable. Learning to do this is the body's only true usefulness."*

So, you will stay on track as long as you keep in mind that the <u>purpose</u> of using the model or the <u>idea</u> of The Chakra System, is to use it as <u>a temporary tool for learning</u>.

And, specifically here, about the Crown Chakra: it can be seen as <u>one</u> expression of an idea that came up in The United Mind - the idea of getting to know Itself in new ways, through the creation of Relationship in Unity between different parts of the Mind, by manifesting Itself in physical forms, different but united. This was a creative and wonderful act, an idea that first brought joy and adventure to Being and Awareness.

What <u>seemed</u> to happen then was the advent of a mad little idea, the idea about individual selves being able to become separated, and when this idea came up, the different parts <u>perceived</u> themselves as separate from *each other and from God. This never happened in Reality, but despite this, the perceived reality immediately led the separated selves to feel guilt and led them into fearing God's revenge, another mad idea completely incongruent with God's nature, which is Love.*

So, the obstacles that for many of you can seem to reside in the Crown Chakra are <u>false beliefs</u> and <u>fear</u>. The methods developed for working with chakra clearing can therefore be meaningfully used, if the false beliefs in separateness and specialness and the fear stemming from these can be cleared out.

What you said about using The Chakra System as a temporary learning tool sounds a bit like when we in our former book "Jesus on Catching the Bull" talked about "the Bull" as a symbol for the separated mind, which in itself is but a symbol and nonexistent as an separated entity, but real and existent in Relationship and Unity. How the Ox-herding Pictures could be of service in the process of Awakening to one's True Self.

Likewise, the Chakra System could be of service to us if used as a learning tool, here for the process of Manifestation of one's Elevated Self in Form.

So, do I understand you correctly when I say that we can use the Chakra System as a workable tool for a while on our Path towards wholeness, but that ultimately we will leave this idea behind us?

Yes and no. Yes, the Chakra System can be useful for a while. But only if you hand it over to The Holy Spirit to use. By yourselves you do will never know for sure how to use it properly, and the ego can take over and use chakra work for its own purposes, like making itself special and "enlightened".

A sobering warning... Thank you, Jesus. So, if I would choose to work with this level, what shall I do?

I am glad that you have laid all hesitation behind you, and now just ask straight-forwardly for my help. It seems like your Facebook message has sunk down into your own sub-conscious mind, as a new and liberating belief:

> *Good morning*
>
> *This is God.*
>
> *Today, listen within, and I will give you a solution for any problem you encounter.*
>
> *You need not figure anything out by yourself, so relax and have a good day!*

Yes, that is a funny thing about beliefs, especially sub-conscious ones: the sub-conscious mind assesses the truthfulness of a statement not from deducing whether in sounds sane or insane, but from how many times it has heard it. This is valid both for limiting beliefs and for liberating beliefs. By being aware of this, one can eliminate negative beliefs and "implant" positive beliefs by consciously "brain-washing" oneself with just repeating what one <u>wants</u> and <u>chooses</u> to believe.

This is partly why A Course in Miracles and A Course of Love are so extensive. The beliefs of the separated mind that are challenged by ACIM are so deeply held by so many, that many repetitions are necessary. And the new beliefs of the Heart presented in ACOL are so revolutionary for the split mind and heart, that they need also to be repeated in many different ways.

But now, back to your question, what you may benefit from doing if and when you choose to work with your Crown Chakra.

As you already have pointed out, the most important thing is being completely Present, for example by meditating, listening inwards to you Inner Silence, and gracefully letting Remembrance of your True Self come back to you.

Good questions to meditate on can be:

- Who am I?
- What is God?
- What is Universe?
- What do I believe?

When you have done this until you feel that your Heart understands these questions, even if your mind still may have difficulties with them, as it always tries to produce "solutions" to "problems", continue with these questions:

- What is my life purpose?
- How do I want to live?
- Whom shall I serve?

For those who like the method Structured Meditation, the one I described in the prologue, these groups of questions can be used as input. And with any method *you choose to use, writing down your thoughts and insights afterwards is always beneficial.*

Another good practice is prayer. In your prayer, try to release any fear that you lack anything, because that always comes from sub-conscious, false and limiting beliefs. Rather, let yourself be filled with the peaceful feeling of being accomplished, the feeling of gratitude from experiencing that what you pray for is already done or is already given to you.

One prayer I proposed in ACIM, a prayer you can use the first thing you do every morning, is:

> *"I am here only to be truly helpful.*
>
> *I am here to represent Him Who sent me.*
>
> *I do not have to worry about what to say or what to do, because He Who sent me will direct me.*
>
> *I am content to be wherever He wishes, knowing He goes there with me.*
>
> *I will be healed as I let Him teach me to heal."*

This prayer has been central for me, and I have used it for a long time. When I now see it in print again, it reminds me of one of the few exercises a reader of ACOL is asked to do (whereas ACIM has 365 exercises):

> "13.2 As you observe, always with your heart and not your mind, and begin to include others in your observation, I ask you to concentrate on one thing only. This is a simple exercise, and enjoyable too. It but calls for you to ask one thing: Ask yourself what you already know of the spirit of the person you observe. You will be amazed at the knowledge you already have and the joy it brings you to remember it.

13.3 These are but exercises in memory recollection, and the more you practice them the more true memory will return to you. Do not apply any effort to these exercises, particularly not that of recalling spirit. Just let impressions come to you, and when they make you feel like smiling know that you are feeling memory return. If, when trying to call up memory of spirit, you find your brow knitting in concentration, you are applying effort and need to cease attempting the exercise at that time. If you give this exercise just the tiniest bit of consistent practice, however, it will soon become routine to you, for you will want to continuously experience the pleasure that it brings.

13.4 While you may desire to put what you feel into words, this exercise is not about putting words on feelings or using them to describe spirit. It is best to leave words off this experience as, if you do not, you will soon be ascribing some attributes to one spirit and not to another, just to differentiate between them. The purpose here is to show you that they cannot be differentiated or compared or defined in the same way you have defined their bodies in the past.

13.5 You will soon find that what you recall of spirit is love. You will want to give it many names at first, and might not even recognize it as love, for it will come without all the longing and sadness you so often associate with it. While the feeling of love that washes over you from one may feel like courage, and from another like gentleness, and while this is all part of what you are encouraged to feel, it is simply asked that you let the feelings come and with them the realization that while no two spirits will seem exactly the same, they also are not "different." The love from each will fill you with happiness because it is already complete and has no needs and so no sense of longing or sadness of any kind. Because it is complete, it will ask nothing of you, but will seem to offer you a warm welcome, as if you are a long lost friend returning home.

13.6 And so you are. This is the new "proof" that, while not scientific or verifiable, will offer you the evidence you seek to confirm the truth of what you are being told here. All that is required to gather this new evidence is to trust in your own heart. Are you willing to believe what your heart would tell you?"

I am glad you chose to include this exercise here - it is very applicable on the level of working with one's Crown Chakra. Opening this chakra up is opening up to Divine Presence and Unity, and Unity is found in Relationship. One of the aims with the exercise is to make the student realize that even if relationships can be experienced as different, they are all still the same - the Relationship with the United Mind, with God. The limited relationship between separated selves is what I call the special relationship, in which love can switch over to anger or bitterness if the "right conditions" are not met. Special relationships are therefore based on fear, even if this at first might be hidden, whereas True Relationships in Unity are based on Love, trust and peace.

I think that we should also explore the inner realm of beliefs. As we said before, you can choose to believe The Holy Spirit, and to trust any inner belief based on belief in Unity with all you brothers and sisters, and thereby with God. The seeming paradox is that the proof of the truth of these beliefs will not come to you until <u>after</u> you have accepted them as Truthful. And what will be frustrating for you is that this proof will be incomprehensible to your mind; it is only possible to be known as True by your Heart. So, what I call you to do is a leap of faith, faith in me.

Isn't this the call of the entire book of A Course of Love?

It is. The ego has severe difficulties with my statement from long ago: "I am the Way, the Truth and the Life", judging it as if I am making myself special. The paradox your separated mind is not able to pass by, is that not until you have accepted <u>me</u> as what this statement declares, are you able to believe in <u>yourself</u>, as the Son or Daughter of God you are, together with everybody else.

And you cannot believe this until you have let go of belief in specialness.

But, talking about letting go of beliefs: the mind believes it has first to find "scientific proof" for falseness before it can let an established inner belief go, and this is what limits and stops you from being who you truly are. Even when your Heart knows that the belief is false, a mind split from the heart cannot and will not know this. But you have taught your clients ways to circumvent the "laws" of the mind, haven't you?

Yes, I have. The method I invite almost all of my clients to use is <u>affirmation</u>, which I talked about before, as a form of "positive brainwash", done by yourself. What I try to ensure when I ask someone to use this method, is that the affirmation that he or she defines really states something the person positively wants to believe, wholeheartedly. In the interactive guide I talked about before, on the internet page http://psykosyntesforum.se/Guide/Guide.htm, there is a specific method for affirmation called The New Record, which can be a good learning tool for those who have not used affirmations before.

Another method, which is based on the fact that inner beliefs are often represented by inner images in one's subconscious mind, is "The Belief Buster", which I will describe briefly here. The method can also be learnt by listening to an audio recording on my web site: http://psykosyntesforum.se/ services_cognitive_script_therapy.htm #Belief_Buster .

First, an explanation about how inner images are built up. The word "image" is normally associated with the visual, but in what I mean with an inner image, it is built up by three different parts: a visual (V), an audial (A) and a kinesthetic (K, body sensations, emotions). So, when I for example say "envision X VAK", this means that you shall "see X within" both with your "inner eyes", hear it with your "inner hearing" and experience it with your body. "X" can be a situation, a person, a place, or yourself. V, A and K describe the different modalities of the inner image, whether it is primarily visual, primarily audial, or is dominated by a body experience, like feeling your body or experiencing emotions.

When I below talk about **sub**-modalities, this stands for all variations that can be made to each modality. The visual content can be seen as a film strip or as a still photograph, seen with colors or black/white, sharp or fuzzy, light or dark, etc. The audial content can be loud or muffled, clear or garbled, close or distant, etc. The kinesthetic content can be painful or pleasurable, weak or strong, vague or distinct, etc.

So, to the method itself:

"The Belief Buster":

a) Think about something positive about yourself that you are convinced of, and that you feel really pleased with. A personal quality, a way of being, a way of reacting, how your self-image is. Envision seeing yourself. Note, and write down, all the submodalities of the visual / audial / and kinesthetic or emotional content that this image, which is your inner representation of your belief of yourself. Note how it feels to say "YES" to this image.

b) Now, think about something <u>negative</u> about yourself that <u>was</u> you, but which feels as if you are <u>not</u> this way at all in your life now, as this is something you have left behind completely. Imagine seeing yourself as the one you were <u>then</u>, and note the differences compared to who you are nowadays. Note, and write down, all the different submodalities of <u>this</u> inner image. Note how it feels to say "NO" to this image.

c) <u>Compare</u> these two inner images with your inner eye, compare your written notes, and write down all the <u>differences</u> in the <u>submodalities</u> of the two different images of yourself. Location, distance, size, still/moving, you are inside the image (<u>associated</u>) or outside looking at yourself (<u>dissociated</u>), contrast, frame or no frame, etc. Compare all the three "channels" separately, the visual part, the audial and the kinesthetic. Write all this down in two columns on a sheet of paper; include also how it felt to say "Yes" and "No" to the images.

d) Now, sit comfortably, close your eyes, and relax. Look at the negative image, the one showing the you who you no longer are. Keep all the submodalities constant, except the brightness. Slowly "turn the brightness knob up" so that the image becomes brighter and brighter, until he whole image is completely white. All the other properties of the image are still there, but <u>the image is empty</u>. If there is sound, "turn the volume knob down" until it is completely quiet. Now reset both the brightness knob and the volume knob to their original settings, but see how the image is now still empty and silent. Let you subconscious mind store this empty frame in your memory as **"The Negative Frame"**.

e) Now let you subconscious mind choose a negative belief about yourself or a negative quality that you <u>sometimes</u> express and that you from your heart want to get rid of, and let your subconscious mind produce an image of yourself having this trait, way of acting or reacting, way of being. Now, quickly insert this image into "The Negative Frame", and see how the image takes on all the qualities, all the submodalities, of this frame. When you now say "NO" to it, with all the passion you can muster, you see how the image of yourself <u>falls out</u> of the frame, <u>backwards</u> and <u>down</u> into a large tin trash can. Hear the <u>crashing</u> sound when the image is <u>shattered</u> to pieces in the trash can. Hear how the lid of the trash can falls down, heavily, with a dull banging sound. Feel your relief, and relax for a while in this nice feeling.

f) Now, look at your positive image, the one showing yourself having a positive trait or a positive belief about yourself, something you really feel pleased with. As before, keep all the submodalities constant except the brightness and the sound volume. Turn the brightness up and the volume down, emptying the image, and then reset the "knobs". Let your subconscious mind store this empty frame in your memory as "**The Positive Frame**".

g) Now let your subconscious mind select a positive trait or a positive belief you <u>sometimes</u> have about yourself, but which you wish from your heart that you could have <u>always</u>. Take this image and quickly insert it into The Positive Frame, and see how the image takes on all the qualities, all the submodalities, of this frame. When you now say "YES" to this image, with all the passion you can muster, you see how the image becomes firmly fastened to the frame, as if glued to it, and how it stays permanently in a frame like this. Imagine going into this image; experience the wonderful feeling of having this with you all the time from now on! Relax for a moment in this nice feeling.

h) Now, return to your inner center, relax, and let your subconscious mind select <u>three more negative</u> traits or limiting beliefs about yourself that you want to let go of, and <u>three more positive</u> that you wish you could have always, and go through the same procedure as above, with these. Take first one negative, then one positive, then one negative again, and so on until you have gone through all six images. Experience fully how it feels to say "NO" to the negative ones, and to experience how they fall out of the Negative Frame and are trashed, and how it feels to say "YES" to the positive ones and experience how they become permanently fastened into a Positive Frame.

i) Finally, when all this is done, now ask your subconscious mind to at the end of each day, when you have gone to bed to sleep for the night, to select one negative personal trait or negative and limiting belief about yourself, and one positive trait or positive belief about yourself that you have sometimes but wish to have always. Ask your subconscious mind to use The Belief Buster procedure during the night, while you are sleeping. Your subconscious mind will not only do this, it will also make you sleep deeper and more soundly than usual, and you will wake up in the morning feeling unusually refreshed and relaxed!

So, this was the "user manual" for The Belief Buster.

Wonderful! I like the way you "fool" the mind by using "inner form" in a novel way. This is a good example of using illusion for positive learning. Limiting beliefs about yourself are from the mind, and even if you in your heart know them to be false, this "inner form" is what controls the mind.

Yes, the mind does not build up inner beliefs from logical deduction and rational thinking. Negative beliefs are to a very large extent built up with emotionally laden inner images that often are formed early in life, often through negative influence from others, like non-seeing parents, harsh teachers, bullying peers, cultural prejudices. The Block Buster works, not by challenging the beliefs in themselves, rather by circumventing them by using the mind's own method of representing the beliefs as inner images in specific ways, with specific submodalities.

I think our readers might find this explanation a bit "engineery", so I would like to urge you, dear reader, to just test the method out and see for yourself. If and when you get your subconscious mind to use it by itself, automatically, you will never again need to consult a psychotherapist!

And put me out of work... But, on the other hand, I know from experience of being a manager that the more I tried to make myself superfluous as a manager, the more assignments I got. I guess that with the same motto, the same thing will happen in my role as a psychotherapist.

It will, in the same sense as what happened when you had managing roles: the way you use your role will evolve.

I just come to think of something, regarding inner beliefs. What if I used The Belief Buster on the negative belief in being a separated self, powerless and a victim of world of danger, lack and pain, and on the positive belief that I am my True Self, in communion with The United Mind and with God?

For you, it would be interesting to see what happens, so try it out!

For those of you readers who have just begun your spiritual journey, I would recommend not to use The Belief Buster as yet on such a deep-rooted negative belief as of the separated self, before you have prepared both your mind and your heart by studying A Course in Miracles and A Course of Love, at least for a while. As I have said, these are required courses. In the introduction of ACIM, I say:

> *"This is a course in miracles. It is a required course. Only the time you take it is voluntary. Free will does not mean that you can establish the curriculum. It means only that you can elect what you want to take at a given time. The course does not aim at teaching the meaning of love, for that is beyond what can be taught. It does aim, however, at removing the blocks to the awareness of love's presence, which is your natural inheritance. The opposite of love is fear, but what is all-encompassing can have no opposite.*
>
> *This course can therefore be summed up very simply in this way:*
>
> > *Nothing real can be threatened.*
> > *Nothing unreal exists.*
> > *Herein lies the peace of God."*

But, when the mind has been prepared, and the split between mind and heart has started to close, The Belief Buster can be a very good exercise for opening up the Crown Chakra. Meanwhile, test it out on other negative and limiting beliefs you may have about yourself!

... ...

(The notation "... ... ..." stands for that there has been a brake in Earth time here.)

I tested The Belief Buster on myself, as I suggested.

This is how it unfolded for me:

a) My positive belief: "I am a good therapist, each time." I see myself as if in a moving wide-screen film, in front of me in the upper part of my field of vision, at a distance of ten feet or so. The image has mild, saturated colors. The image is surrounded by a thin golden frame. I hear sounds, but no distinct words. I feel how the atmosphere is calm, secure.

b) My negative belief about one thing I have left behind me: "The Noble Victim". I see him as a tense, insecure, stern-looking young man. He stutters sometimes when nervous, he dislikes himself, tries always to please. I see the image as a black-and-white photo to my left, just outside my normal field of vision, at a distance of thirty feet or so, framed with a black, thick edge. No sounds. I feel how my shoulders become tense when I look at it; I feel a knot in my stomach.

c) I compare these two images:

The Negative Frame	The Positive Frame
V: Wide-screen high-resolution film with beautiful colors, near, up in front, thin golden frame.	Black-and-white blurry photo, outside field of vision far away to my left, broad black frame.
A: Soft voices, but no distinct words.	Silent.
K: Peaceful atmosphere.	Tenseness in shoulders and stomach.

d) I empty the Negative Frame, just keeping the thick black frame and all other submodality properties of the original image.

e) I choose a negative belief I sometimes carry: "I am separate from everyone. I was born alone, and I will die alone. I am a powerless victim of the circumstances of my life."

I see myself in the Negative Frame, and I feel tense and unhappy. But, I say "No!", and I see how the picture falls away and down, I hear it shatter in the trash bin, the lid closes tight with a thump. And I feel deep relief, I sigh, breathing out completely. Both literally and symbolically...

f) I focus on The Positive Frame, again seeing myself at my work. Turning brightness up, sound volume down, I empty the Frame, and then I reset the brightness and sound again. I see the empty golden frame, a warm white area within.

g) I choose a positive belief I wish I could have always: "I am part of God. I am one with Him and with all my Brothers and Sisters. I share with them life's abundance. I will live always. I am."

I see myself in The Positive Frame. The colors are vibrant. In my heart, I know this image will stay there, fastened to the beautiful golden frame. I see myself surrounded by people, a friendly smile on my face. I hear them speak, I hear no distinct words, but I sense that they speak calmly, how they listen to each other, a peaceful dialogue.

I feel how I relax, how my shoulders relax, my breathing deepens. I feel how I smile…

Thank you Lars for sharing this. I sense that for you, so often identifying yourself with your thoughts and your thinking abilities, this exercise works on a different level.

It really does. I wonder why I haven't thought of using it myself before, instead of focusing on teaching others.

Maybe the right time was just now.

When you say that, it feels like the word "maybe" was inserted there just to hide the fact that you knew…

No, I didn't. As I said before, until you know truly who you are, you will not share completely who you are, and therefore I cannot "read your thoughts". What I implied with the word "maybe" was that you in your Heart maybe knew that this was the right time.

You are right. Thank you for your patience with me…

Again, as I said before, I am outside of time, I need not be patient. On the contrary, I feel joy when you make discoveries like this one!

… … …

... ...

When I came back today, I came in anger.

At the same time, in wonder - I have experienced this
so many times: when I open myself up to the Divine,
my ego, the collective ego, whatever, immediately
strikes back...

In a conversation yesterday evening with my wife and
my youngest son, where we were discussing an
application for a change of courses he was going to
hand in to the school, I remembered the last day for
handing in the application incorrectly, and my wife
scolded me angrily in critical terms: "You never listen
to what I say, you don't show me respect by not even
trying! Shouldn't you write about that in your books?"

This triggered my hurt ego, and I lashed back,
scolding her for showing me lack of respect in front of
our son.

In my anger, I slept on a sofa during the night, and I
was still angry when I came to my office. I had
planned to continue writing, but with the angry mood
I was in, this felt impossible. Instead, I sat down in
my therapist's arm chair, closed my eyes, and
thought about what I had written in this chapter and
which contrast there can be between lofty thoughts
about Divinity on one hand and real life on the other.
I remembered the exercise about focusing on the
spirit of another person, and I attempted this with my
wife. This made my anger abate, and after a while the
thought came "I really should know better than this...
but I don't... so please, tell me what to do!"

Immediately, the answer came: "You needed to give her feed-back about her bitterness, but you could have done it differently, and at a better time. Ask her to forgive you your anger."

At once, I felt completely at peace. But, still a little apprehensive to just talk to her on the telephone, I sent her a sms, where I asked her for forgiveness, and suggested that my anger might have been at myself, thoughtlessly forgetting things.

Soon, I got an answer, where she accepted my apologies, and then she just continued to chat about every-day things like what the dog just had done. She concluded by expressing worry about my declining memory. Which felt a little annoying, but I'll soon forget that... ;)

Thank you, Jesus, for reminding me like this that the Divine and the mundane need to be in constant relationship!

In this case, don't thank me. I could well have done it, but this time it wasn't me, it was your own Self doing the whole job, and a good lesson it was, I hear!

Yes, in all its trivialness it was. First, it taught me to never stop watching out for my ego, it will take every chance...

Secondly, I learned that I am on my way on "Catching my Bull" better and better - I scolded her, but I did it from my need of setting appropriate borders, and I could refrain from saying anything personally insulting, which well could have happened when I was younger.

Thirdly, I learned how anger, even when it is triggered by a petty incident like this, really eliminates my inner peace completely. And I learned how much I value this inner peace. Nothing is really worth more than having it and staying in it.

Without inner peace, you cannot listen inwards. If you cannot listen inwards, you will not hear the silent language of your Heart. If you cannot listen to your Heart, you will not listen to me, and you will be on your own. On your own you are at your ego's and others egos' mercy. And the ego has no mercy.

On the other hand, if and when you listen to your Heart, and you act on what you hear, inner peace is inevitable.

You make it sound so simple... And I recognize, for the thousandth time, how my mind and my ego complicate things, and how my Heart makes them simple...

But, to now start to conclude this chapter on the Crown Chakra, what can be said more?

Looking at the table of the chakras again, the dominant element is said to be "information". Could one say that opening up the Crown Chakra is important in order to get "True" information, instead of getting the ego's "information", which is based on illusionary things, for example one's limiting negative beliefs?

	Name	Location	Element	Color	Qualities
	Crown	Top of the head	Information	Violet	Awareness, Knowledge
	Third Eye	Centre of forehead	Light	Indigo	Perception, Imagination
	Throat	Base of throat	Sound	Blue	Communication, Creativity
	Heart	Center of chest	Wind	Green	Compassion, Relationship
	Solar Plexus	Solar Plexus	Fire	Yellow	Will, Spontaneity, Self-esteem
	Sacral	Beneath the navel	Water	Orange	Feeling, Pleasure
	Base	Perineum	Earth	Red	Trust, Stability, Grounding

Yes, that can be said. The mind can produce much useful information, but it takes the Heart to <u>decide</u> which of the information that can be used for True Service, which is the only thing that always benefits everybody.

So that is why the table includes the qualities Awareness and Knowledge at this level?

Yes. Awareness and Knowledge about one's True Identity. It is when you lose contact with this

*Awareness that you may fall prey to the "demon" on this level: **attachment**. Attachment to form can lead to many excessive characteristics like over-intellectualism, spiritual fundamentalism and confusion. It can also result in obstacles like learning difficulties, spiritual skepticism, limiting beliefs, materialism and even apathy.*

You make it sound like a life or death thing...

It is, quite literally. As I said already two thousand years ago:

> *"Very truly I tell you, I am the gate for the sheep. All who have come before me are thieves and robbers, but the sheep have not listened to them. I am the gate; whoever enters through me will be saved. They will come in and go out, and find pasture. The thief comes only to steal and kill and destroy; I have come that they may have life, and have it to the full."*

This, I both think and feel, is an appropriate ending of this chapter! Real Life is a life in Union. Union is first experienced through the Crown Chakra. The experience of Union needs then become deepened and manifested.

Let us continue to the next chakra, The Third Eye.

2. The Third Eye.

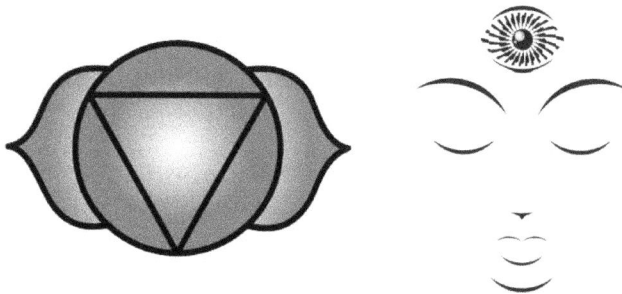

The second chakra from the top is The Third Eye. It is located at the center of the forehead.

The primary question at the level of the Crown Chakra was "**Why?**" - Why am I here? Why need I open up upwards?

And the shortest answer is "To know who I am in Truth".

If the Crown Chakra question is **Why**, the primary question of the Third Eye is "**What?**" - What is it I want to manifest here? What is my Vision?

The seeming coincidence that the word Vision can stand for both my inner images of how I want my life to be, and stand for my ability to see, is meaningful.

The Third Eye can be said to stand for True Seeing, in contrast to what the body does, using the physical eyes and the visual decoding function of the brain, which is perception.

The element for the Third Eye, in the table above of the chakras, is light. But not light in form, which science describes as an electromagnetic waveform or as small particles, photons, depending on how one "sees" light with measuring devices. Rather, the Light as described in Lesson 108 of ACIM:

> "True light that makes true vision possible is not the light the body's eyes behold. It is a state of mind that has become so unified that darkness cannot be perceived at all."

The Third Eye has been a very popular symbol in many occult teachings, and has been said to be connected to the pineal gland, the only non-paired part of the brain, located at the top end of the spinal cord. The philosopher Decartes believed the pineal gland to be the connection point of mind and body, but he was also the origin of a central idea of our culture - "mind and body". This is a misconception scientifically refuted by the neuroscientist Damasio, who has proven that the brain and the body are both needed in building up what we call intelligence, which includes both mental and emotional intelligence. The reason the pineal gland has been associated with the concept of the Third Eye is probably the fact that this gland controls the hormone melatonin, which is connected to biorhythms for night and day.

Here, the concept The Third Eye will be used as a symbol for the state of mind "that has become so unified that darkness cannot be perceived at all".

This state of mind is one where one has contact with one's intuitive and creative abilities. The intellect, the "rational" mind, can be creative, but here I will use the terminology of ACIM, where it differentiates between "creating" and "making". What we create belongs to Truth, what we make is just made up, illusionary.

By using the body´s eyes, or only one's brain's visual center, one can see things externally and also see ("visualize") imagined things. In ACIM's terminology, we by this "make" things, either the external physical world, or the inner imagined world. ACIM states furthermore that there is no real difference between these two, the external world is but a projection of the inner world we make up:

> "Projection makes perception. The world you see is what you gave it, nothing more than that. But though it is no more than that, it is not less. Therefore, to you it is important. It is the witness to your state of mind, the outside picture of an inward condition. As a man thinketh, so does he perceive. Therefore, seek not to change the world, but choose to change your mind about the world. Perception is a result and not a cause."

So, in the terminology used here, this is the important difference between imagination on one hand, and creation and creative imagery on the other. Through imagination we make up illusions, which we perceive as "real". Through creation, which always is co-creation with God, we create True Reality, which we see with True Vision.

The idea of The Third Eye will thus be used here as a symbol of our ability for True Vision.

So, do you agree with my explanation, or rather, my definition?

I do, even if I myself would have described it in a more condensed way.

With all due respect, dear Jesus, having read what you have authored so far, I doubt it.

Touché... But, this was <u>defining</u> the concept. What are your ideas about how to <u>work</u> at this level, how to open this chakra up?

Another way of defining The Third Eye could be to see it as representing the power not only to See Truly, the power of Vision, but also the power of <u>En</u>-visioning, using it for Creative Imagery.

Yes, that feels useful! In my mind, creation must start with <u>envisioning</u> what one <u>wants</u> to create. But wait - how can one distinguish the difference between envisioning and just making things up, imagining? Again, I feel weary about how one's ego can sneak in and take things over...

And you are correct in feeling weary. The ego can take over and it will, if it gets the slightest chance. But, you can rest in peace; there is a simple instruction on how to avoid this:

You <u>cannot</u> envision anything by yourself. As soon as you try to, the result will be imaginary. At best, the results will be harmless and temporary. At worst, the result can cause harm and suffering for yourself and others, but also in these cases, it will be temporary.

By using the Vision of The Holy Spirit, you can envision truly. What you then will envision, will be a co-creative act together with the United Mind, and what you thus envision will benefit everybody.

If you rely on your mind only you will not be able to distinguish between imagining and envisioning.

But, if you let yourself sink down into your Inner Silence, and listen to your Heart, you will know. When your mind and heart are united, and both speak the same language, the first necessary condition for True Creation is met: True Vision and True Envisioning.

So, by myself I cannot do anything. It is only by asking for help that I can. Sounds a little diminishing...

Lars, dear friend - that is the voice of your ego. In listening to your Heart you are not asking someone else for help - when you truly listen, you are in contact with, you are your True Self.

To your ego this is bound to sound as arrogance. But, as I said in ACIM:

> *"The Voice of the Holy Spirit does not command, because It is incapable of arrogance. It does not demand, because It does not seek control. It does not overcome, because It does not attack. It merely reminds. It is compelling only because of what It reminds you of. It brings to your mind the other way, remaining quiet even in the midst of the turmoil you may make.*
>
> *The Voice for God is always quiet, because It speaks of peace. Peace is stronger than war because it heals. War is division, not increase. No one gains from strife. What profiteth it a man if he gains the whole world and loses his own soul? If you listen to the wrong voice you have lost sight of your soul. You cannot lose it, but you cannot know it. It is therefore 'lost' to you until you choose right."*

I teased you before about authoring lengthy texts... I take that back - my experience again and again is that every word in ACIM and ACOL is necessary and indispensable.

For some they may all be useful, but I have said in ACIM that anyone can, at any point in the course, reach a point of complete insight, which I describe as:

> *"There is no need to further clarify what no one in the world can understand. When revelation of your oneness comes, it will be known and fully understood."*

But, back now to my question, how is one to work with this level, if one wants to See instead of perceive? What are your ideas about this?

The first idea that comes to my mind is a tool I often use in my therapeutic work, Visualization or Guided Imagery. Roberto Assagioli, the founder of Psychosynthesis, said about visualization (Psychosynthesis 1965):

> "The imagination, in the precise sense of the function of evoking and creating images, is one of the most important and spontaneously active functions of the human psyche, both in its conscious and in its unconscious aspects of level."

> "Every image has in itself a motor-drive."

> "Images and mental pictures tend to produce the physical conditions and the external acts corresponding to them."

Assagioli implicitly differentiates between the "imaginary realm", which is what we make up, and the **"Imaginal Realm"**, which can be seen as a level of reality between the United Mind and physical reality. In the Imaginal Realm, the "Information" (the element of the Crown Chakra) is starting to take on form with the element Light (the element of this chakra) in the process of envisioning.

On my company website there are a number of visualizations recorded as digital audio files, and which I think can be beneficial for training one's ability for creative imagery and for opening up The

Third Eye:
Deep Space, The Church, The Cocoon, The
Encounter, The Gift and The Water Lily (see
http://psykosyntesforum.se/ps_visualizations.htm.
Newsletter subscribers can listen online for free.)

*Yes, these exercises can be very useful. Creative
imagery is not a personal trait, even if some can do it
easier than others, it is a skill. Being a skill, it can be
trained.*

*There is one danger though in imagery and visualizing
what you want into your life. I think you just read
somewhere something like this, which emphasized the
importance of having a vision:*

> *"Vision without action becomes just a daydream.
> Action without vision can become a nightmare."*

*But, the danger with visualizing is that when you are
doing it, you are somewhere else, you are not present.
After envisioning something, in order to move towards
manifestation, concrete action is needed. And to act
without being present is to be like walking with your
eyes closed - you are bound to stumble.*

*With this, it is like so many other aspects of life on
Earth - everything has to find its natural rhythm,
whether it is your breathing, your being awake and
asleep, activity and rest, doing and being.*

*You need to find your own rhythm for listening
inwards, and then for manifesting outwards. A daily
discipline for training Inner Vision at certain times can
be good. You can for example include exercises for
opening up The Third Eye in periods for morning and
evening meditation.*

But is what The Third Eye symbolizes, True Vision, to be used only when envisioning things? I thought that the goal of both ACIM and ACOL is to reach a state where True Vision completely replaces perception.

Thank you for bringing that up. Of course True Vision is what you should have, both when envisioning, visualizing, creating inner images of your Vision, and when you act in the world and relate to others.

These are but two different applications of True Vision. Using True Vision is to see with the "eyes" of The Holy Spirit, who can see both the divine and the mundane.

So, in addition to using True Vision, The Third Eye, for "inner seeing", practice using it with your physical eyes as well! I think your little e-book Conscious Vision can be a helpful tool in this.

Wow, I never thought my products would get divine endorsement...

You forget what I said on the Mount a long time ago, about prayer: "Your Father knows what you need before you ask him."

Even when my needs are commercial in nature???

Of course. The only thing that matters in using things in your physical world, is what you use it for. If you let it be a tool for the Holy Spirit to use, it becomes service. If you let your ego use it, use can even turn into abuse.

In this specific case, I think that if the exercises in your eye and vision training program can enhance peoples' abilities to become and stay present with What Is, this would be a good thing.

Many of you may think you are aware of what you are looking at, but very often what you see is merely your projections, which are colored by your memories, preconceived notions, prejudices, beliefs, and so on. This is why I said "Let the little children come to me, and do not hinder them, for the kingdom of God belongs to such as these" - small children have not yet lost their ability to see clearly.

OK, thank you for your recommendation. Here is the link to the course, which I now give away for free, as a kind of pay-back for your endorsement:
http://psykosyntesforum.se/
PsF_0883_Conscious_Vision/
PsF_0883_Conscious_Vision.html

And, as long as we are talking about training courses around seeing and vision, I might as well mention the e-course **"My Mission"**, which includes a large number of exercises and visualizations around envisioning the Purpose of one's life and one's visions of this. I think this e-course could constitute an in-depth training of The Third Eye.
http://psykosyntesforum.se/courses_my_path.htm.

These two e-courses are in a way both about seeing, the first on about seeing externally, the second one more about looking inwardly.

Good! And as I said, you need to find your natural rhythms for when to use True vision in these two ways. And note - there are more than one rhythm going on simultaneously:

- *One happening in seconds and minutes, while you are seeing a Brother or Sister, in one moment with your physical eyes, in the next moment with your Third Eye, seeing his or her Spirit.*

- *One happening over a period of hours, when you are active in the world, <u>doing</u>, and then meditating or contemplating, <u>being</u> with yourself.*

- *One happening over periods of months or years, in the gradual awakening process towards realizing your True Identity, sometimes in reclusive Stillness, sometimes manifesting it in action.*

The first one in your list is what we within Psychosynthesis call developing "bi-focal vision", the ability to see <u>both</u> another person's personality with all its positive and negative traits, <u>and</u> his or her Spirit, or Higher Self to use the Psychosynthesis term.

Yes, and this is the true base for Forgiveness - seeing that the former belongs to the world of form and therefore is a product of projections, and the latter is the True Identity of the person, and therefore the only aspect of a person that is Real.

But, this will come up later in this book, I think, when we will talk about The Heart Chakra.

We have up to now talked some about how to work with The Third Eye, and about the importance of clearing any obstacles on this level, in order to achieve True Vision in the present moment.

Now it may be appropriate to again talk about the other ultimate purpose of opening up The Third Eye, specifically in the context of this book - becoming able to envision yourself as Elevated Self in Form, creating an Inner Vision of this.

The Vision Statement

Thank you for reminding me! My "inner engineer" lets itself be so caught by methods, tools and other "fun stuff", so I sometimes forget <u>why</u> we are doing this exploration.

But is there a United Vision, or how should we approach this area?

I have described <u>my</u> vision of what we can do together here on Earth, before God takes the last step and brings you all Home to Him - The Happy Dream. But each of you needs to envision your <u>individual</u> part in this, create a Vision of your own how you in your life wish to see your own ultimate goal of becoming an Elevated Self in Form. I suggested in the first chapter that you meditate on the questions

- *What is my life purpose?*
- *How do I want to live?*
- *Whom shall I serve?*

Now may be the time to, with the help of your Third Eye, and with the help of the tools and methods described above, to create an Inner Vision of how you want <u>your</u> answers to these questions to look like.

In my e-course I mentioned above, "My Mission", I offer tools for creating Vision and Mission statements.

In this course, I emphasize the importance of not only visualize a Vision, but also to verbalize it, and when doing this, to follow these instructions:

- Formulate it in present tense, as if your Vision has already been achieved. Include yourself in your **Vision Statement**. Describe the Vision in itself, not how to come there.

- Formulate your Vision in positive terms only, what you want to happen, how you want it to be. The goals shall feel attractive and they shall feel "right".

- Be precise and concise. Make one description of each aspect of your Vision. Use as few words as possible. Be specific, but not limiting. Use a "reality connected" language: describe what you see, hear, touch, describe how your body feels, thoughts and emotions.

- Use power words: "have", "can", "master", "own", etc. Avoid fuzzy expressions like "want to achieve", "will strive for", "will fight for", etc. Reflect: What would you rather - strive for a good relationship, or have a good relationship?

- Use words that activate thoughts and emotions that increase you inner energy: courage, willpower, acceptance, intelligence, love, happiness, peace.

- Formulate in a way so that you do not unnecessarily activate limiting emotions connected to needing control, needing acknowledgement, needing security.

Good advice. How does your own Vision Statement sound?

Ouch, you caught me there... I have thought about it, but I haven't actually verbalized it. As you said, I am probably writing this book much for my own sake, as a way of taking steps forward on my own journey. So, let me ponder on this...

... ...

Verbalizing my Vision was rather difficult - there came a lot of resistance from my ego, and typical inner criticism like "who do you think you are..." and the like. I must admit that it took some courage to write down my dream of how I wish my life to be, in an uncensored way.

> "Both in my professional and in my private life, I am led by The Holy Spirit. I can always hear the voice of the ego when it comes in me or from another person, and I am each time able to choose again, and to listen to my True Self instead.
>
> Through my encounters with others, I experience how the message from A Course in Miracles and A Course of Love is taking root in more and more places, both in the corporate world, in study groups, and among people active in traditional religion.
>
> I have found peace in the inner conviction that I need only be my Self to truly serve - 'I need do nothing'."

Thank you, Lars, for your courage to be so honest and open with your dream. Maybe your honesty and openness will be contagious, and will make others dare to dream as well.

Allowing oneself to dream is the same thing as allowing oneself to hope. To allow oneself to hope is what I have called "a little willingness", willingness to have faith. Willingness does not arise from conviction but brings conviction. By verbalizing your dream, and thereby envisioning it inside, you are both expressing and experiencing your willingness to be open to that it is possible to reach.

And I assure you, the more of you that are willing to dream like this, the nearer the Happy Dream will come! Because, the Happy Dream is not only possible, it is inevitable. What your dreams do is saving time.

So, this far, do you feel we have covered enough aspects of working with The Third Eye?

I think so. But, before continuing to the next chakra, The Throat Chakra, I would just like to include a quote from ACOL, where you speak so beautifully about vision and imagery:

"You have no capabilities that do not serve you, because they were created to serve you. The ability to imagine is such a capability, freely and equally given to all. Imagination is linked to True Vision, for it exercises the combined capabilities of mind and heart. It is akin to perception, and can lead the way in changing how you perceive of yourself and the world around you.

Beyond imagination is the spark that allows you to conceive of what never was conceived of before. This spark is inspiration, the infusion of spirit. Taking the creation of form backward, it leads to this conclusion: Spirit precedes inspiration, inspiration precedes imagination, imagination precedes belief, and belief precedes form."

3. The Throat Chakra.

The Throat Chakra is located at the base of the throat, at the shallow cavity just below the larynx with the medical term "the suprasternal notch".

The element connected to The Throat Chakra is sound, and if the action of the chakras above were the "inner actions" of becoming aware and of envisioning, the action of the Throat Chakra is the "external action" of communication, communicating yourself and your visions to others. If the Crown Chakra was about **Why**, and the Third Eye was about **What**, the Throat Chakra is about **How**. How can I express who I truly am? How can I reach out?

Once upon a time, in a time before time, we humans sat around the fire, warding off the darkness. On long winter nights, we told stories to keep ourselves connected to the past, to the future, and to each other. We told stories of how the world was created, why we were here, and where we were going. We told stories to our children, and they told stories to their children, on through countless generations. These stories have become real for us, and from this reality, we have created our world.

In the context of this book, The Elevated Self in Form, opening up the Throat Chakra is to tell a new story, the one about who you really are, about how you see your Brothers and Sisters in Christ, about what our world can become and how we can create it together. Communicating this new story is the first step towards manifesting one's True Self.

But, having come this far in my introduction of the Throat Chakra, I become uncertain. Again, how can I be sure that what I communicate will help, that it will further my dream of a better world? How can I be sure my ego doesn't take over, and uses communication to impress, to convince others to believe in my message, to inflate myself?

Your uncertainty is justified, but is a good thing that you "Catch your Bull", your eager mind, before it starts to make things up. But this far, I think your description of The Throat Chakra is good, and I really like your metaphor about "telling a new story".

As I have said before, whether anything in form is meaningful, and communication through speech and writing is form, depends on what you use it for. In ACOL, I warned:

> *"When one thinks, 'There is so much to say', one forgets to listen. Be guided in your going out. Be restrained in what you say. Be attentive in your listening.*
>
> *Where you are is where you are supposed to be. The path to follow to all changes will be shown to you if you will but be attentive. If you follow the way that is shown to you, all uncertainty will end."*

So, is what you are saying that communication in itself is meaningless if it is not part of a dialogue?

You are on track. "Communicating in dialogue" can be seen as a synonym to the word "relating". And you are not a separated self, you <u>are</u> relationship. Relationship to the Christ in your Brother and Sister, to God. And being in relationship <u>is</u> to communicate, even when you don't talk.

And, as soon as you communicate, as soon as you relate to another person, you get feedback. If you listen, feedback will lead to experience. And, it is only through experience True Learning can come.

Furthermore, about listening: if you listen with your heart as well as with your mind, you will hear when feedback is from the ego of others, or if it is God speaking through them. By recognizing the source of the feedback, both types of feedback are useful for your learning.

But, back to the topic of this chapter: The Throat Chakra. We have been discussing communication in general. The Throat Chakra is also connected also with speech itself. The content of the communication is not the only thing revealing the origin of communication, whether it comes from the ego or from the Self. By paying attention to your own voice and that of others, the quality of the voice can reveal much.

I haven't thought of that. How do you mean that this can be heard?

All forms of fear reveal themselves in for example a tense voice, a shrill voice, hoarseness from using too little air or too much air.

And if I notice this in my own voice, what should I do?

This is an interesting thing about the body, and a good example how to use it as a learning tool: what the body does but reflects what's going on in the mind. If you use your mind to change what is happening in the body, the feedback from the body will change the mind.

So, if you with your mind influence your body into relaxing, this will affect your state of mind.

Oh, I see what you mean. I just came to think of an exercise I originally developed for my stuttering clients, The AOM Breathing. In this exercise one can learn how to achieve instantaneous relaxation through a very specific breathing technique. This exercise was and is very helpful for them in re-discovering their ability for fluent speech.

After a while, I discovered that this breathing technique was very beneficial in other types of problems as well - all psychological problems where fear was involved and where the anxiety attack was one of the prominent symptoms.

The technique is inspired by the Hindu tradition of AOM meditation, and I think that there is a strong connection between breathing and spiritual development. In Christian tradition, one talks about "the Breath of God" that gave life.

So, from what you said I can see how one by using a technique like the AOM breathing can change one's state of mind from being fearful to becoming peaceful. For those of our readers who want to test this, here is another free give-away:

http://psykosyntesforum.se/
PsF_0882_Breathing/
PsF_0882_Breathing_1.html.

Yes, this will certainly work. And by finding your Inner Peace, you will start to listen inwards again. And by listening inwards, listening to your Heart, and through this to The Holy Spirit, you will realize that there is nothing to fear. As I said in the beginning of ACIM:

> *"When you are afraid of anything, you are acknowledging its power to hurt you. Remember that where your heart is, there is your treasure also.*
>
> *You believe in what you value. If you are afraid, you are valuing wrongly. Your understanding will then inevitably value wrongly, and by endowing all thoughts with equal power will inevitably destroy peace.*
>
> *That is why the Bible speaks of 'the peace of God which passeth understanding'. This peace is totally incapable of being shaken by errors of any kind. It denies the ability of anything not of God to affect you.*
>
> *This is the proper use of denial. It is not used to hide anything, but to correct error. It brings all error into the light, and since error and darkness are the same, it corrects error automatically."*

So, an important part in opening up the Throat Chakra can be to find one's deep and relaxed breathing and then to speak with a steady, calm voice?

Surely. And your e-course can be a good learning tool for this, because the foundation of voice is breath.

But, going back to the content of communication. I know you teach communication skills, both in groups and with your clients. I have gathered that the concept you have developed is based on the fact that people often project out their beliefs onto the world, and that they then perceive them as belonging to their external reality.

Yes, I do. I call this concept Basic Communication, and it is available as an e-course: http://psykosyntesforum.se/ courses_basic_communication.htm.

In this course, one can learn to become aware of one's own way of communicating, as well as others'. And one can learn how to use a new structure for how to communicate one's inner world and one's emotions with greater openness and honesty. And also how to communicate clearly how one is aware of the three "worlds" involved in all types of communication between people: my external <u>physical</u> reality, my inner <u>mental</u> reality, and my inner <u>emotional</u> reality. How these three different realities are located in different places: outside of me, in my brain, and in my body. And what can happen when I confuse these with each other, and/or do not communicate clearly which one of these I am talking about in each moment.

It is my impression that when you succeed in using your own concept yourself, which I know you have become better and better at, through teaching it, you talk more "from your heart" than "from your brain".

You are probably right. I think when I use Basic Communication myself, I stop telling others what to do, and instead, I "tell the story about myself" in a way that does not attack. I am able to communicate my thoughts and interpretations in a humbler way, in a way adding "this is what I think, but correct me if I'm wrong". I am also able to tell others what I need with "a straight back", without criticizing others for their needs, even if these get in conflict with mine. If needed, I negotiate, but Basic Communication helps me to avoid power struggles, rather it helps me to create an I-thou attitude were the negotiation instead becomes a joint effort to find a win-win agreement.

So, if we would sum up what we have talked about here, and make a list of what one can do to open up one's Throat Chakra, how would that list look like?

OK, let's try to do that. But first I would like to clarify what type of communication I think this list shall be about. We often need to communicate in order to relay information, like when buying a newspaper, or agreeing on a time for a meeting, or informing people at a meeting, and so on. This is communication needed for practical things, and seldom causes problems or conflicts.

What I would like to sum up here is what may be important when communication is more part of relating: letting yourself be known, trying to get to know the other person, communicating thoughts, values, beliefs, emotions, needs, and so on.

- Before you talk, listen first. Both to others and to your heart. "Catch your Bull" - stop yourself when you sense that you are listening to your ego.

- Communication is more than words. Practice AOM Breathing, so that you talk from a state of inner peace.

- "Tell your story": communicate what <u>you</u> are experiencing, what <u>your</u> thoughts are about this and how you interpret it, and how this makes <u>you</u> feel.

- Facilitate dialogue: <u>ask</u> the other person about "his or her story". Listen without judgement.

Do you want to add anything to this list?

Just one more thing, a reminder, something we have not talked about explicitly in this chapter, but which is central:

- *Communicating is relating. Relating is responding. Whatever happens, respond by extending Love. Meet fear with Love, meet attack with Love, meet Love with Love. Unconditional Love is the only answer you need.*

This last point may seem difficult at times, and your ego will surely make it difficult, by judging. But, <u>if</u> you have succeeded in opening up your Crown Chakra, letting The Holy Spirit in, <u>and</u> succeeded in opening up your Third Eye, seeing things with True Vision, <u>then</u> what comes through your Throat Chakra cannot be anything else but Love.

You make it sound as if this was easy…

It is! Complication is of your ego mind. Your ego <u>wants</u> things to seem complicated, in order to convince you that its own "solutions" are the only ones that will *work. Your ego even regards Unconditional Love as both arrogance and as naïveté. But, the world you perceive is but witness to the ego's "solutions". Unconditional Love <u>is</u> the only thing that <u>will</u> work.*

If you listen to your Heart, you know this.

Yes, I do. I really do...

The Mission Statement

But, one more thing. We have talked about opening the Throat Chakra in order to be able to communicate honestly and clearly. In the context of becoming an Elevated Self in Form, we should also talk more about "telling one's story", of stating the Personal Mission one may have defined for oneself, describing <u>how</u> one intends to reach one's Personal Vision, which we talked about in the former chapter.

Later in this book, we will be talking about will-power, in connection to the chakra Solar Plexus. There I will describe a model of the willing process, where the first step is setting a goal. In the context of Elevated Self in Form, the Personal Vision is an expression of this goal. The willing process also includes the step "affirming the goal", and one part of this affirming is to openly express <u>how</u> one intends to come there, one's "Mission Statement".

In the e-course "My Mission" that I have mentioned a couple of times, there is an instruction on how to design one's Mission Statement in such a way that it meets certain criteria I deem as important:

1. SHORT: The Mission Statement shall preferably consist of one single sentence, or at the most three short ones.

2. EASY TO UNDERSTAND: It shall be possible for a normal twelve-year-old to immediately understand it.

3. EASY TO REMEMBER: If you were to be awakened in the middle of the night and asked to present your Mission, you shall be able to say it by heart, without time-delay or hesitation.

Furthermore, an efficient Mission Statement shall include three things:

1. The **activity** needed: three verbs.

2. **What** you offer, promote or create.

3. **For whom** this is aimed.

Having defined, verbalized and expressed your Personal Mission, especially when you pronounce it using your voice, will energize you.

In the e-course My Mission I give a number of examples of well-known Mission Statements that meet many of the criteria I set up above. For example, even if I don't know if they were intended to be actual mission statements, I have used quotes assigned to you:

”The thief comes only to steal and kill and destroy; I have come that they may have life, and have it to the full. I am the good shepherd. The good shepherd lays down his life for the sheep.” (John 10:10-11)

”I am the way and the truth and the life. No one comes to the Father except through me.” (John 14:6)

The first quote is taken out of its context, and was not meant as a mission statement, even if I certainly described what I saw as my mission at the time.

The second one, on the other hand, I can see as being a Mission Statement, although I don't think it met the second of the criteria you set up: easy to understand. It has been misunderstood, as I talked about in the first chapter, and has been interpreted as if I was making myself special. The good thing about the statement is that it did meet the other two criteria: short and easy to remember.

But I am pleased you chose it as an example, and your choice made me ponder on how I would have expressed it today. I think my new version could be like this:

> *"I am a Son of God. I am the way and the truth and the life, because when I have awoken you into remembering that you are the same as I, you will unite with our Father, and with me."*

Thank you, Jesus. I am awed by the fact that you are not "ready" with all your thoughts, and that you can let yourself be inspired by <u>me</u> into formulating new ideas!

It's OK for you to respect me, as an older brother (well, OK, much older), but reverence is not warranted. We are but brothers engaged in a dialogue, a creative process, where we can create, as the equals we are.

But, I know for a fact that you, in contrast to your Vision Statement which you had not formulated, have a written Mission Statement since many years, and which you described for example in your e-course "My Mission".

Yes, I do. Originally, I intended it to be about my professional life only, but now when I read it again, I realize that I maybe formulated a Mission Statement for my whole life:

> "My Mission is to
> teach, inspire and coach
> those wanting to find their True Self
> to let go of what stops them from seeing."

When you read this now, would you agree with me that for example writing this book is a part of your Mission?

I agree. And I feel thankful for having become inspired (as used in the meaning "divine influence") to formulate this Mission Statement, because I think that even if I have not thought about it in a conscious way for a long time, it has guided me sub-consciously.

One could even say to our readers, in the hope of tempting them to do this: opening your Throat Chakra, and using it to communicate your heart-felt Mission Statement, will influence you more and deeper than you may realize.

To this I would like to add: an open Throat Chakra will also help you to "tell your story" in a way that reveals your Elevated Self in Form to others.

But now, let us continue to the next level: The Heart Chakra.

Let us do so - this is my favorite level!

4. The Heart Chakra.

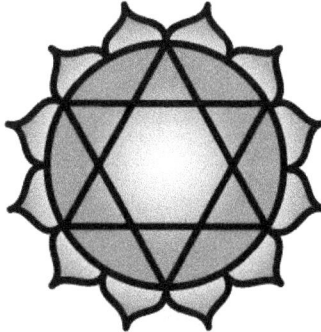

The Heart Chakra is the midpoint in the system of seven major chakras, and is in this <u>the balance point</u> between spirit and matter, mind and body, heaven and earth.

The element associated to the Heart Chakra is **wind**, or **air**, and this symbolizes that this chakra is connected to both breath and our relationship with everything, our <u>interconnectedness</u>. We breathe to get oxygen, which would not exist without trees and plants, and they in their turn depend on us through the carbon dioxide we exhale.

Opening the Heart Chakra is to become aware of the fact that we don't need to do things by ourselves. Through relationship, partnership, collaboration, we can do more with less effort, as we then tap into the power of the United Mind.

The chakras above are connected to the questions **Why**, **What** and **How**. The Heart Chakra is about <u>relationship</u>; the central question here is **Who**. <u>Who</u> is the person I am relating to; <u>who</u> am I, relating? <u>Who</u> do I <u>want</u> to be?

The Heart Chakra is connected to all that which is "heart-felt", both in oneself and in relation to others: **acceptance, forgiveness, generosity, care, gratitude, compassion, love**.

By listening to your heart you get immediate <u>access to</u> simple and workable solutions, whereas the mind will often over-analyze and provide complication and "solutions" that do not serve all involved.

But foremost, in the context of this book - how to manifest one's Divine Self in the world - the Heart Chakra is connected to the Calling of the Heart. Opening the Heart Chakra, listening to one's Heart, is to hear this Call.

The Calling of the Heart

I quote what ACOL says about this, as I felt it really "spoke to my heart" when I first read it:

> "Having a calling is often spoken of in lofty terms. Few outside of those who feel they have a calling for something beyond their ordinary, limited, view of themselves use this phrase. But many recognize that they have a calling even unto things the world considers mundane.
>
> How does a farmer explain that she or he cannot be other than a farmer? That rising and setting with the sun is in their blood, in the very nature of who they are. That being one with the land is essential to them.
>
> What bravery it takes in today's world to follow a calling to teach. To set aside other careers that offer far more prestige and economic gain to instead be a sharer of knowledge, a shaper of minds. What overriding

kindness calls one to take care of another's body, to be a healer? How does one explain a joy that is like no other and that comes from the simple act of caring for a child, preparing a meal, bringing grace and order to a home?

This list of different callings could be endless, and each could be considered unexplainable. Those who seek an explanation before following a calling, who look for reasons of a practical nature, who would seek guarantees of the rightness and outcome of following such a call, seek for proof they have already been given. The call itself is proof. It is proof of the heart's ability to be heard. Of the heart's ability to recognize the unseen and to imagine the existence of that which will reveal its true nature and its joy.

All of you are capable of hearing the truth of what the heart would tell you. All of you are just as capable of believing in that truth as of doubting it. All that prevents you from believing in truth is a mind and heart acting in separation rather than in union."

When I read this again, I can really feel how I long for hearing this Call. Then, at the same time, I recognize how my life all the time becomes filled with other things - practical day-to day issues, problems, "relationship friction" - all kind of obstacles, diverting me from listening to my heart.

I feel that most of us understand the vital importance of why we should strive for opening up the Heart Chakra, and that this insight can act as a reminder, making us try, but how can we learn to really do it?

Good introduction to the area of the Heart. I know that you know that this really is a central issue for me, and I am pleased that the passage you quoted spoke to your heart.

The Calling of the Heart is not only a calling to <u>do</u> something, it is a calling for you to recognize and <u>be</u> your Self, your True Identity.

On your question on "how" there are of course a multitude of answers, where different methods or approaches suit each one differently. Let us together explore whether we can find things that may work for many.

I would like to, a little arbitrarily, start with a word you mentioned above: "interconnectedness". You mentioned it in connection to nature, and I think this for many could be a good initial way of opening up one's heart: experiencing the interconnectedness with nature, by going out to some beautiful place and just enjoying <u>being</u> there. As the element of the Heart Chakra is wind, just experiencing a gentle summer breeze against you skin, if done with mindfulness, can become a strong "heart opener".

I love how you always seem to be able to make things simple. When I posed the question on "why", <u>my</u> thoughts immediately drifted away to complicated visualization and meditation techniques...

Acceptance

But, is not the heart connected to relationship? It seems to me that being alone out in nature could even distance oneself from relationship.

That is a very valid objection. It can, but only if you see nature as something outside of yourself. My advice is to focus on experiencing your <u>relationship</u> with nature, <u>accepting</u> your complete interconnectedness with all *there is, and accepting the fact that you and everyone else are part of it.*

It is often easy to find acceptance of the nature, especially nature that has not been altered by man. Imagine yourself being at such a place.

Visualize your acceptance of how it is around you as a golden light inside your heart. Feel how this acceptance, accepting and loving all around you, to be an indispensable part of Universe, makes you full of light, energy, warmth. Imagine yourself slowly letting this light expand, until you are completely inside a sphere of light, and feel how you completely accept and love yourself, knowing that you are a priceless Son or Daughter of God.

Continue to expand the sphere of light, until if encloses everyone you know, and feel how you accept them completely, as the Divine Beings they are, how your love extends to them, just in this moment. Expand the sphere of light more and more, including also all the people you do not know, even the ones you have never met, until the sphere of light encloses all Earth.

Continue, let the sphere of your light enclose the Sun and the planets, then the whole galaxy The Milky Way, then all the other galaxies, wider and wider, until all of universe is inside your sphere of light. Feel the Inner Peace of Complete Acceptance and Love.

... ...

Thank you for this wonderful visualization. I really felt how a thing like acceptance doesn't need to come from intellectual understanding, it just comes from the heart, as a natural state of mind and heart in union.

But, how about the other "heart energies" I mentioned above: forgiveness, generosity, care, gratitude, compassion, love? Is it enough envisioning oneself taking these on, as inner qualities?

Envisioning oneself having them is a good start, but this is as you use to say to your psychotherapy clients: "Insights are good, but they do not by themselves lead to inner change".

Many of these inner qualities can, and need to, be cultivated and practiced to grow. All of the ones you listed, with the exception of love. Love cannot be taught, because it is beyond teaching. But if you take away obstacles to love, if you open up your Heart Chakra completely, love will flow out as the natural part of you it is.

So let us take each one of the other ones at a time, and talk about how one can make them grow by practice in concrete action. How about forgiveness? I read somewhere about resentment, that harboring it is like "drinking poison and hoping that the other person will die".

Forgiveness

Yes, resentment is a common obstacle, which one may need to let go of. Forgiveness will make this possible, but one needs to realize the difference between real forgiveness and mere condoling.

True forgiveness can occur when you no longer see yourself as a victim, and when you can let what has happened be just a neutral, albeit a negative, memory.

Before you are able to do this, the inner wound you experience needs to be healed. For this to happen, appropriate anger may need to be expressed, and then released. Tears may need to be shed, your pain may need to be expressed and witnessed.

When all emotional clearing is done, and when one has become reconciled with what has happened, forgiveness will complete the healing, both of yourself and of the person you have forgiven.

So, if I make an inner inventory of my resentments, and then contact each one involved, forgiving each one, will that work?

You say it is good to simplify things, but sometimes one can over-simplify. Firstly, all your resentments are not in conscious awareness. You may need to train your self-awareness in order to spot these hidden resentments. They may show up in some stray words, seemingly harmless, but both the quality of your voice and the reaction of the one "hit" by your comment will reveal your underlying resentment.

And keep in mind, "huge" resentments are not worse than "small" resentments, both are equally much obstacles to your inner peace. You need to uncover all, and this may take considerable time. But, I promise you, this is time well spent, because your salvation depends on your doing this thoroughly!

And secondly, everyone may not be ready to accept your forgiveness, or may not even understand what you are talking about. But this is not an obstacle to your forgiveness - you need only forgive completely in your heart, and even if you never say anything to the person, forgiveness will happen. Not only for you, but in the other person's experience as well, albeit sometimes subconsciously. When this happens, you may experience it as a miracle, and this would be an appropriate reaction from your side, because this is an example of a miracle proper.

You have clarified this often before, but this really needs to be repeated. Thank you!

But, another thing about forgiveness. I live in the country of Sweden, and one central part of our culture still is what the Norwegian author Aksel Sandemose called "The Jante Law", where one is expected to feel shame about one's shortcomings. Degrading oneself, feeling shame is almost seen as a virtue. Is forgiveness of oneself also important?

It is not only important, it is vital. If you cannot forgive yourself, you will not be able to accept forgiveness from others, and you will probably have difficulties in forgiving others. There is also a risk that you suppress your shame from your conscious awareness, and project your hidden guilt onto others, judging them instead. Just as a reminder, this was what you did originally, which led to the making up of your whole world.

If you harbor shame, in any form, even seemingly mild, make this affirmation a daily practice:

> *"I have made human mistakes,*
> *which have caused pain and sorrow.*
> *I have learned from these, and I forgive myself.*
> *I am a sinless Child of God, who loves me.*
> *I forgive myself, and I trust God will lead me."*

… … …

I practiced your affirmation. Thank you from my heart for it - I realized that, contrary to what I believed, I still had hidden guilt and shame, because affirming the forgiveness for myself and affirming God's love for me felt so healing...

I really understand why ACIM talks so much about forgiveness, and why it is repeated again and again - unforgiveness, for oneself and for others, really goes deep. Judgement and unforgiveness really are two of the ego's most viscous weapons, which can close the Heart Chakra completely.

It feels like we could continue talking about forgiveness for ever. But for readers of this that feel a need of exploring the power of forgiveness more, I recommend reading A Course in Miracles. I just scanned it for the word "forgive" and got almost 1000 hits...

On the other hand, in the sequel to ACIM, A Course of Love, I found "only" 65 instances of "forgive", which I see as a sign than ACOL regards forgiveness as a sufficiently completed lesson, assuming that the "pupil" has done his or her homework. A reassuring sign telling me that this journey is a worthwhile one.

The typical engineer, making mathematical statistics of spiritual development... no offence though ;)

No offence taken! I know, maybe these numbers mean more to me than others. But having read both of the books numerous times, I base my observations not only on the numbers, they just confirmed my feeling.

So, let us leave forgiveness for now. How about the next of the "heart energies" on my list, generosity and care?

Generosity and care

For most people, just deciding to be generous and caring is enough, as this decision implicitly can be a decision to stop listening to one's ego and instead listening to one's heart.

But, even after deciding, the ego can still take over. It can make you seem generous, but as a hidden agenda it strives for making others dependent by having to "pay you back". The ego can make you seem caring, but only in order to impress others.

So, one may have to practice <u>unconditional</u> generosity, <u>unconditional</u> caring. But as your poet Rabindranath Tagore wrote: "I slept and dreamt that life was joy. I awoke and saw that life was service. I acted and behold, service was joy!"

With this, I hope I have tempted you, dear reader, to experiment with things you maybe don't usually do. Give away something you planned to sell. Volunteer in a nonprofit organization you believe in. Talk longer than expected to a stranger you meet while waiting for the bus. Even if you cannot help, show that you care for someone's suffering. Even if you are tired after work, show your partner or child that you care by being present, focused and listening.

It feels good to hear you <u>tempt</u> with something that most people in our culture regard as sacrifice.

Generosity and care have nothing to do with sacrifice. Sacrifice, even if it has been judged by you as "noble", has but two negative net effects: <u>you</u> will ultimately feel resentment, <u>others</u> will ultimately feel guilt. None *of you will benefit from this, on the contrary - in the long run it will make you both sick.*

Unconditional generosity and care fulfil not the "laws of the world", but they fulfil the "Law of God", which says that giving and receiving are one. The only true way to happiness is service.

In my heart I believe you, but I can hear my ego protesting...

The Heart Talk

I came to think of a practice in which one can practice generosity and care in a somewhat unusual way. It is a practice called "The Heart Talk", and I have used it as a consultant at work places where I have been consulted to help them with internal conflicts. The practice is simple but has shown to have profound and positive effects. The format I used was like this:

I bring a small red heart made of soft velvet. I hand it to one of the participants of the group I am here to work with, with the following instruction, which is also put up on the wall in written form:

    a) Each one receiving the velvet heart, can either choose to talk, or can say "I pass", and hand the heart over to the next person in the circle.

    b) If one chooses to talk, <u>one shall talk from one's heart</u>. What is said shall be only about oneself, and shall describe one's own thoughts and emotions around the situation in focus. The words "you", "he", "she" or "they" shall be avoided.

c) In the telling of "one's own story" there shall be no comments on what others in the group have said before in this meeting.

d) All the ones listening shall do this without any comments, questions or any other interruptions.

e) The person talking shall be allowed to speak uninterrupted until he or she is finished, which is signaled by handing the velvet heart over to the next person in the circle.

f) When everyone has received the velvet heart, we shall thank each other for our generosity of our time and for that we all have shown that we care for each other, by listening without judgement.

This practice sounds like a very good way of opening up the Heart Chakra in everyone involved. The format also sounds like it would be useful in other contexts as well, like in families.

It probably would, but I have never had the chance to try it there. I would like to invite the reader of this book though, to experiment with this format in any context involving more than two persons, and where more "heart energy" could be needed.

But, to continue: how about gratitude then?

Gratitude

The ego focuses on lack, and on the future, planning on how to get what it lacks. Or it focuses on the past, resenting how it has been bereaved or has been stopped from getting its "fair share".

By focusing on everything in your present life that you <u>have</u> and that you feel grateful for, you open up your heart to the present.

The reason the ego cannot do this, is because it perceives the present as just a "passing now", something that immediately belongs to the past.

The heart knows that the present is the Eternal Now, and Presence is Being in this timeless place, Being outside of time.

So, start off your day by thinking of everything in your life that that you have now and that fills you with gratitude. Dwell a moment on each thing, on each person involved, and experience the gratitude, as the heart-felt feeling it is.

End each day with the same exercise, this time adding your gratitude to God.

… … …

When I just now did what you proposed, I immediately came into a warm feeling, and I felt peace... It disturbs me how my ego so often succeeds in making me forget the obvious, that I have so much I feel grateful about.

Yes, actually <u>letting</u> oneself <u>feel</u> gratitude is different from <u>thinking</u> that one <u>should</u> feel so.

But this is only one of many important aspects of gratitude - openly <u>expressing</u> one's gratitude to others also opens up one's heart, and it will open up the other person's heart as well.

I work with relationship coaching, and I have heard so often how every-day routines often make us take others for granted. And even when one remembers to <u>feel</u> grateful, we forget to <u>say</u> it. And the fact remains - none of us are mind readers...

I think that if you remember to express gratitude over even small things that your partner, or your colleague, or your friend has done for you, you will not only make him or her feel good about themselves, your gratitude will be contagious. Gratitude will spread like rings on a water surface.

Yes, in this aspect gratitude, like all other "energies of the heart", follows God's Law - when you share this energy you have more of it for yourself. The ego's laws, in contrast, say that what you share leaves you with less.

And the ego prides itself to be the rational one, and accuses the spirit to be an irrational dreamer... and by this missing out on millions of win-win deals! Talk about being stupid...

I prefer to use the word insane. It might sound worse, but it also implies that even the ego is free of sin, whereas saying that someone is stupid is a judgement. Remember: "Forgive them, for they know not what they do". This goes for your ego as well!

Thank you for reminding me, again, that there is no evil, there is only fear. And fearfulness can make us greedy, wanting, resentful, even hateful.

Can one even say that practicing to feel and to express gratitude makes us saner?

If you but look at the state of your world, the answer to your question should be self-evident...

But to put this in correct proportions: what we have been talking about here is happening in many places. Many are awakening to these simple but profound truths, and experiencing concrete effects of following these practices. As I have said before, much waste of time will still occur and much suffering will still plague you, but the ultimate complete return of sanity is inevitable.

Compassion

I choose to believe you, and this choice makes me feel calm, even if I often also feel sorrow about all the sad things happening in the world, about the appalling insanity.

But, to continue with the "energies of the heart" - compassion. This seems to be a central issue of all the big world religions. To quote Dalai Lhama XIV:

> "If you want others to be happy, practice compassion.
> If you want to be happy, practice compassion."

Compassion is a central issue, together with acceptance, forgiveness, generosity, care, and gratitude. The world religions put slightly different emphasis on them, but in all teachings, all of these are central. It is important though to remember that all of these "heart energies" emanate from love, and they can be seen as but different expressions of love.

When you reach the awareness of your True Self, that you _are_ Love, united with all your Brothers and Sisters and through them with God, all these "heart energies" will be part of your natural way of expressing your Self, and of your natural way of relating to others.

Without compassion, you will not know who you are yourself, and you cannot know another person except superficially.

But before we continue to see what can be said about compassion and how to cultivate it, we need to define the word more precisely. Compassion is connected to empathy, but the notions empathy and sympathy are sometimes confused.

Empathy is to feel _for_ and _with_ someone. Sympathy is to feel _as_ someone. Even if sympathy can feel nice, and can feel as if you are compassionate, feeling sympathy is more like recognizing yourself in the other person and feeling as him or her. This can give understanding, but there is also a risk for "becoming caught in the other's story" - sharing his or her beliefs, interpretations and values. If the suffering of the other person is even partly a result of erroneous beliefs, faulty interpretations of what has happened or muddled values, sharing these might not be helpful, it can even make things worse.

Compassion, on the other hand, feeling empathy, is to feel _for_ and _with_ the person, but without becoming caught in his or her ways of thinking and feeling. As you do not confuse who you are in relation to the other, you can be helpful. You can be gentle and caring without reinforcing things that only increase the suffering, rather by being clear about yourself and by being present you can be truly helpful.

To be completely sure that you use empathy in a helpful way, let The Holy Spirit guide you, as I explained in ACIM:

> *"To empathize does not mean to join in suffering, for that is what you must <u>refuse</u> to understand. That is the ego's interpretation of empathy, and is always used to form a special relationship in which the suffering is shared. The capacity to empathize is very useful to the Holy Spirit, provided you let Him use it in His way."*

I agree with you completely in this. As a therapist, I know that burn-out is a common risk for many in my profession, and I suspect that this may partly be a result of confusing sympathy and empathy.

This was an issue for me in the beginning of my career as a psychotherapist. As a way of supporting myself in remembering to avoid this confusion, I composed an affirmation, where I used two words that seemed to be in opposition: non-attachment and empathy. Non-attachment can be a good thing, but has also a quality of distance, lack of contact. I combined these into a "new" quality, which I then cultivated, by affirming "<u>nonattached empathy</u>".

This helped me to observe the person and the person's story without judging and without jumping to conclusions. It helped me to stay clear about myself, and to keep "my own story" out of the way, my own experiences resembling those my client spoke about.

It also helped me to stay nonattached to a "desired result" of my therapeutic interventions; rather I could trust the person's <u>own</u> ability to find out what to do, with the help of the tools and ideas I provided. Often, what my client came up with was unexpected to me, and gave much <u>better</u> results than I had anticipated.

Good and useful observations. At the same time, I think that it is not only the tools that you provide that produce positive results - the <u>relationship</u> between you and the client is probably the dominant factor. With the risk of sounding disrespectful, one could even say that "therapy is what you and your client occupy yourselves with in order for your True Selves to get the opportunity of create healing without becoming disturbed by the rational mind".

No, I don't think that is disrespectful at all. At least not for one who believes what you say in ACIM:

> "Ideally, psychotherapy is a series of holy encounters in which brothers meet to bless each other and to receive the peace of God. And this will one day come to pass for every 'patient' on the face of this earth, for who except a patient could possibly have come here? The therapist is only a somewhat more specialized teacher of God. He learns through teaching, and the more advanced he is the more he teaches and the more he learns. But whatever stage he is in, there are patients who need him just that way. They cannot take more than he can give for now. Yet both will find sanity at last."

But, back to how to open one's Heart Chakra by cultivating one's ability for compassion. What can we say about this?

Your Christian religion, as well as other religions, have emphasized sacrifice, and as I said before, this is not only unnecessary but it is even harmful. It has also emphasized compassion, but often in connection with sacrifice, or putting one's own needs aside.

To be compassionate in a helpful way, you may have to first learn how to become "selfish in a sound way". A person who is selfish in this way, firmly believes the following, an affirmation I know you often teach:

> *"The needs of others <u>and</u> my needs are important.*
> *I can meet others' needs <u>better</u>,*
> *if I <u>also</u> meet my own."*

In self-sacrifice, one prioritizes the needs of others above one's own, and one will not be able to be truly helpful in the long run.

In egoism, the needs of oneself are prioritized, and one does not want to help lest there is some gain for oneself.

This sounds like a dilemma. How does one avoid either of these extremes?

By becoming aware of the needs, both one's own and those of the other person. In this, one has first to be aware of the fact that there is often a gap between what someone says that one <u>wants</u> and what one truly <u>needs</u>.

Secondly, in order to know and understand the needs, you have to <u>listen</u>. Both inwards, listening to your heart, and outwards. This way you can differentiate your needs from the needs of the other person, and avoid projecting your subconscious needs on others.

What you say here reminds me of a communication structure I teach in my course Basic Communication, where I talk about how to communicate in a negotiation. The structure is called Basic Negotiation, and is based on a model of the human psyche I call The Onion Model:

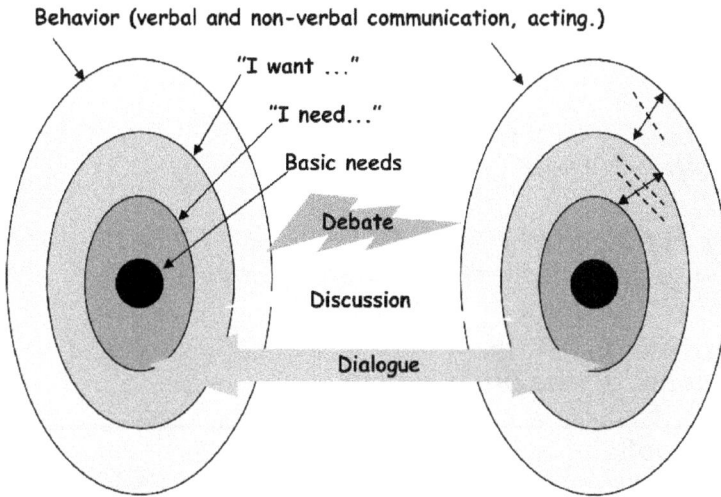

Behavior (verbal and non-verbal communication, acting.)

"I want ..."

"I need..."

Basic needs

Debate

Discussion

Dialogue

In this course, I essentially say that you may not be able to feel compassion and empathy for what a person <u>does</u> or <u>says</u>, or what he or she <u>wants</u>, but if you understand the true <u>needs</u> of the person, you <u>cannot</u> do anything else than feel empathy.

But to reach this understanding, you need to pass by the stages "debate" and "discussion" in your communication, which are where the mind often ends up. Instead, if you listen to your heart, you can come to "dialogue", in which both you and the other person dare to and are able to be open, honest and trusting.

(Read about this at <u>http://psykosyntesforum.se/courses_basic_communication.htm</u>.)

But, after having read what I just wrote, I feel that this context, trying to reach an agreement with someone, is rather limited. Empathy is of course important in this context, but I realize that compassion may be important also when not trying to reach an agreement, or when one is not able to "do" anything about the situation.

Your input here is very useful despite this. In brief, your structure for negotiation is:

1) <u>Listen</u> *until you understand the true needs of the other person.*

2) <u>Express</u> *your understanding, your acceptance and your respect for these needs.*

3) *Listen inwards, and then clarify your <u>own</u> true needs to the other person.*

4) *Negotiate.*

In all encounters, even those that have nothing to do with solving a problem, negotiating an agreement, or the like, point 1 and 2 above describe a structure for being empathic and compassionate, and <u>expressing</u> it. Even if the last two points are not applicable to the situation, what you have done so far may be very helpful.

Your structure also points at the importance of being <u>present</u>. Without this, you cannot truly listen. As soon as you are "somewhere else", in your thoughts remembering thing resembling the present situation, or in your thoughts planning on what should be done, you are not truly listening.

One can say that showing compassion and empathy are synonyms for <u>being with</u> the person, whether you are able to meet needs or not.

The word "compassion" comes from Latin and means "being <u>with</u> someone's suffering", and "empathy" comes from Greek and means "feeling <u>with</u>".

I expressed this in ACOL like this:

"It is the relationship inherent in meeting another's need that makes the meeting of the need a thing of lasting value. It is your willingness to say, 'Brother, you are not alone' that is the benefit of such situations, not only to your brother but also to you. It is in saying, 'Sister, you are not alone', that spiritual hunger and thirst is met with the fullness of unity. It is in realizing that you are not alone that you realize your unity with me and begin to turn from fear toward love."

So, to sum up all that we said here about compassion, it seems to me that if I open my heart to someone, by staying present in the Eternal Now and by listening with awareness and patience, compassion will be the inevitable result.

This is true. But at the same time, I would like to remind you that the ego, both your own, the one of the other person, and the collective ego, will try to divert you from this, as unity for the ego is experienced as a threat.

This is why I have emphasized that Seeing truly, which is another way of expressing Being with, is a <u>decision</u>. A decision you may have to make again and again. I said in ACIM:

"If I see nothing as it is now, it can truly be said that I see nothing. I can see only what is now. The choice is not whether to see the past or the present; the choice is merely whether to see or not. What I have chosen to see has cost me vision. <u>Now I would choose again, that I may see.</u>"

As a psychotherapist, I take comfort in my knowledge about the subconscious mind: what it has <u>heard</u> enough times is "true", and what it has <u>done</u> enough times becomes an automatic response. If one is diligent in being aware and staying present, and one makes the choice you talk about enough times, even this will become an automatic response.

Heart Breathing

Up to here, we have focused only on mind and heart oriented ways of opening the Heart Chakra. As a closing of this chapter, here is a powerful technique which includes the rest of the body as well:

I.   **Heart focus**: Close your eyes, and focus your attention on your heart, and the area around it inside your chest. Holding a hand on the area can make it easier to focus.

II. **Heart breath**: At the same time as you keep focusing on your heart, imagine breathing "through" it. Breath in slowly during five seconds, hold your breath for three seconds, breath out calmly during five seconds, hold your breath for three seconds. (During learning to breathe like this, counting 5-3-5-3 may be helpful.)

III. **Heart feeling**: Keep your focus on your heart, feel as if you are breathing through your heart, and ask yourself: "How do I most of all want to feel now? What emotion, what state of mind, do I want the most, just now?"
Experience how now, when you breathe in, you receive this feeling from the Universe. Holding your breath, experience the gift of this feeling. Breathing out, give the Universe this feeling. Holding your breath, feel how it is received, as

your gift. Continue to receive and to give,
experience your total interconnectedness with
All.

This focus / meditation / breathing technique has
been proved to increase and stabilize the Heart Rate
Variability (HRV), which has been scientifically shown
to have significant impact on both physiological and
psychological well-being.

To measure your own HRV, and to train Heart
Breathing via bio-feedback, see
http://www.psykosyntesforum.se/bio_feedback.htm.

*This is another excellent example on how to use your
body, thoughts and emotions in close connection to
each other as an efficient learning device. This practice
is a good way of uniting body, mind and heart into
what I call wholeheartedness.*

*To be compassionate as God is compassionate is to see
as God sees. Again, I stress to you, this is not about
looking upon misery and saying to yourself you see it
not. I am not an advocate of heartlessness but
wholeheartedness.*

I explained the word wholeheartedness thus in ACOL:

> *"It can come as no surprise to you that your mind has
> ruled your heart. What this Course has thus far
> attempted to do is to briefly change your orientation from
> mind to heart. This is a first step in what will seem now
> like an attempt to balance two separate things, but is
> really an attempt to unite what you have only perceived
> as separate.*
>
> *If the heart is the center of your Self, where then is the
> mind? The center is but the Source in which all exist as*

one mind. To say this to you before we loosened some of your perceptions about the supremacy of the mind, however, would have been folly. The one mind is not as you have perceived your mind. The one mind is but a mind in which love rules, and mind and heart are one.

We will proceed by calling this <u>wholeheartedness</u> rather than mind or heart."

I cannot find much more to add about the Heart Chakra after this...

Except just repeating what I said in the very beginning of this chapter:

The Heart Chakra is the midpoint in the system of seven major chakras, and is in this <u>the balance point</u> between spirit and matter, mind and body, heaven and earth.

So, with this we will continue one level down again, now to the chakra Solar Plexus.

5. Solar Plexus.

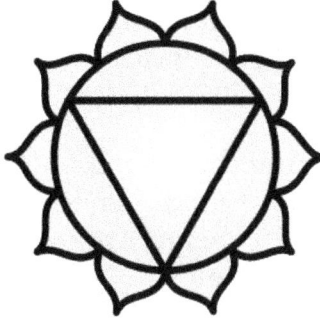

The chakra **Solar Plexus** is situated at the navel. The element of Solar Plexus is **Fire**, which can be seen as a symbol for the power of **Will**, and for **Courage**.

… … …

... ...

I find myself just sitting here, contemplating what to write in this chapter, but getting nothing done. First, this surprises me, as the writing of the chapters above felt inspired, swift and effortless.

Then, it dawns on me that Fire is the Element in my Elementity Profile that I express less than the others. Fire, Will Power and Passion are qualities I since long know that I need to develop.

My primary Elements are Earth and Water. Earth represents the engineer side of me - rational thought, logic and order, stability and security. Water represents the therapist side of me - relationship, listening, flexibility, harmony, good will.

Now you maybe understand why you are writing this book - even if it hopefully will be useful for others, the writing of it is helpful to you, just now.

As you now enter the lower half of your journey down through the Chakra System, things are getting more physical and practical in a more concrete way. You have opened up to Divine Intention through your Crown Chakra, you have visualized your goal with your Third Eye, you have communicated your mission through your Throat Chakra, and you have extended love and compassion through your Heart Chakra. These are all necessary for a full life, but they will not by themselves get the job done.

What job?

Why, saving the world, of course ;)

I can still feel how my ego cringes at the hubris it thinks your statement reveals, even if you say it with tongue in cheek. But, I know that you are also serious - our mission is to save the world. And taking on a mission takes willpower, lest it just remains as an idle dream. Something needs to happen. I suspect that this is what this chapter shall be about - how to make things happen.

You said once "Seek not to change the world but choose to change your mind about the world." And you also said "You need do nothing". I recognize that these statements are about becoming aware of how one's ego always wants to do something, how it always wants to correct what it sees as faulty.

And I know that when you talk about saving the world, you mean that by saving ourselves, by remembering who we really are, Sons and Daughters of God, we also become able to perceive our brothers and sisters as such, thereby helping them to ultimately come to the same realization.

And I know that remembering who I really am is remembering to "choose again", to choose the voice of The Holy Spirit instead of the voice of my ego. Both are eternally present, but the ego's is louder...

Choosing again is the same as deciding, vigilantly deciding for the Kingdom of God, deciding against the kingdom of the ego. And decision-making takes will-power.

Good! You really have made your homework, son!

I would like to add something about will-power. Many of you have struggled with the seeming contradiction of how God wants you to have free will, and how I want you to listen to God's will. Many of you have felt that the latter feels like having to obey, to surrender, to sacrifice what you want for yourselves.

This paradox is resolved when you realize that listening to The Holy Spirit instead of listening to your ego will <u>free your will</u>. Using your will-power to decide this will <u>liberate</u> you into uniting your knowledge with mine and therefore <u>uniting</u> your will with mine. When you do this you will have no sense of sacrifice, it will not feel as surrender, this I solemnly promise!

But, I also know that this takes a leap of faith, and that just <u>before</u> making the decision, it will probably feel as surrender, each time. This is why it takes will-power, and as a psychotherapist you have surely experienced how your clients have been able to make important decisions regarding their lives, and stick to them despite intense anxiety and inner resistance.

The ego will not only use its thought patterns to stop you from deciding for God, it will use emotions as well, especially an emotion like bitterness. Bitterness is to your heart what ego thoughts have been to your mind. And the ego wills this, and the will-power of the ego is tremendous! With its will-power, it has created the world you see, a world with perpetrators and victims, with suffering and resentments, with anger and bitterness.

The three aspects of Will

In Psychosynthesis we talk about the three aspects of the will: **Good Will**, **Strong Will** and **Skilful Will**. I agree with you about the large will-power of the ego, but it seems to me that this will-power is concentrated on Skilful Will, which can be used for manipulation, and on Strong Will, which the ego uses for bullying people into following its "orders".

Yes, you are right. This is the central characteristic of the ego - it lacks Good Will, it doesn't even know what it is. It can <u>seem</u> to express good will, and it will try to convince you of its good intentions, but there will always be some gain for itself lurking behind.

Good Will comes from the Heart. This is why I in ACOL talk so much about the necessity of becoming "whole-hearted", where mind and Heart are united.

But, Strong Will and Skilful Will are neutral forces in themselves. They can be <u>used</u> by the ego, which often leads to <u>abuse</u>. On the other hand, <u>if</u> you let your Heart always <u>decide</u>, letting your Good Will take the first step, <u>then</u> you can let your Strong and Skilful Will <u>serve</u> you and others. They have then to be used in balance, and always from a decision from the Heart's Good Will.

Their service to you and to the world can be enhanced by training the will-power, as long as you do not let the ego usurp your increasing ability to influence. This last warning is unfortunately warranted - there have been many well-intentioned persons, who on their spiritual path have trained their will-power, becoming very charismatic and influential, but who eventually have become dominated by their egos' will-power. Many manipulative and suppressive sects have come into existence out of the ego's usurping an originally divine intention. But: "By the fruit you know the tree".

Can one train one's Good Will?

No, Good Will is of the Heart, and by this its source is The Holy Spirit. It needs not be learned or trained, it needs only be remembered, as your heritage, as a Treasure within yourself.

As soon as you can stay in this remembrance, training your will-power with respect to Skilful Will and Strong Will can enhance your ability to be of service to God, to be an increasingly useful Miracle Worker.

The psychology you have as your professional base, Psychosynthesis, is sometimes called "the psychology of the will". I am sure you know of many tools and methods for training the will, don't you?

I do. The founder of Psychosynthesis, Roberto Assagioli, even likened the Will to a muscle, something that you can train to become stronger, and which on the other hand will wither if not used.

First, I would like to include here his model of the Will, which he introduced in his book The Act of Will, and which I have elaborated on in my e-course "My Mission" (http://psykosyntesforum.se/ courses_my_path.htm.)

The Act of Will (The Will Process)

1. **Set the goal**. In the context of this book, this is the same as visualizing yourself as Elevated Self in Form. This inner image needs to be concretized:
   What is it I want to value?
   What self-image do I want to have?
   Which inner beliefs do I want to guide me?
   Which skills do I want, which of those I have may need to be developed more?

How do I want to <u>act</u> in the world?
In which <u>contexts</u>, situations, with whom?

2. **Deliberate**. Many stride into action too soon, and deliberation is important, especially if the goal is, as here, a life goal, something which may be life-changing. Deliberation can be done in many ways: meditating, contemplating, discussing with others, reading about others having set similar goals, et cetera.

3. **Decide**. After having set the goal, and deliberated on it (which may have led to alterations and/or refinements of the first Vision and Mission Statements), it is time to make a conscious decision. To give it energy, it is often good to express it openly, to others or at least to yourself, using the power of your Solar Plexus, making your voice forceful. In the pronunciation of you decision, use "energy words" as **"I will ..."**, **"I intend to ..."**, etc. Avoid "fuzzy" expressions like "I will try to...", "My ambition is...".

4. **Affirm**. After having come to your decision and expressed it verbally, the decision needs to be grounded fully into your whole body, mind and emotions. It needs to become <u>heart-felt</u>. You may need to energize courage, having "the guts". This can come out of pronouncing your Vision and your Mission openly and clearly to yourself and to other people, with a voice supported steadily by your diaphragm (Solar Plexus energy). You can also formulate an affirmation, where you say **YES** to your Vision and your Mission.

5. **Plan**. Assagioli probably meant, when using this word, more "common" goals in life. In such a long-

term goal as striving towards a Personal Vision via having formulated a Personal Mission Statement, you may not be able to do a concrete step-by-step plan. But, to at least have a general Action Plan is crucially necessary, even if it probably may have to be revised now and then over time.

With a good Action Plan you can relax and find an inner state of openness. This inner state implies

- I am receptive to important feed-back from others.

- I will discover possibilities instead of seeing problems.

- My intuition and gut feeling will guide me forward.

- Seemingly accidental but deeply meaningful and helpful things will happen more and more often.

6. **Act**. A common shortcoming is to set goals, refine them, decide to pursue them, talk about them, but then to get stuck in "preparing" and not acting. The only thing that counts is going from words to deeds! Courage is not a description of someone free of fear - courage is acting <u>despite</u> fear.

If inner resistance overcomes you, ask yourself:

- In which situations do I march in step with others? Why?

- Who will by themselves give me the permission to walk some other way?

- What would I do if I was ten times braver than I believe I am today? Could I do it anyhow?

And remember: Your Mission is part of a bigger

one. You need not have everything needed yourself, you need not know everything yourself, you need not take everything into account before acting. You are a <u>channel</u> for power, energy, and knowledge. You can connect with the Source of this by going into yourself and turning upwards.

7. **Evaluate**. This is a step that Assagioli did not include in his description of the Will Process, I have added it. The reason for including it is my experience (especially from times when I worked as a Project Manager) that things <u>never</u> turn out as planned. This is an axiom, which is necessary to accept - plans always need to be revised, things often have to be done again, or new things need to be added. But even if this is the way it is, having a plan is always better than acting without a plan. Evaluating your plan afterwards will make you put together a better plan next time.

Also, evaluation is crucial for learning - reflect on everything you know and now can: is not at least 90% a result of learning from mistakes you have made?

This concludes the description of the Will Process, as defined by Roberto Assagioli and elaborated by me as an adaption to the context here, becoming An Elevated Self in Form.

I like the clarity of this! It makes me think of what I said on the Mount: "Simply say 'Yes' or 'No'. Anything beyond this comes from the evil one", with whom I of course meant the ego. In the will process, the ego will always try to complicate things, especially when you listen to your heart. Here the ego's hidden message will always be "seek, but do not find". It will also try to throw you off your Path with emotions like fear, anxiety, uncertainty, feelings of inferiority, and so on.

Except for inner resistance, you didn't talk much about negative emotions in your description of the Will Process. As you work with people's emotions all the time, you have tools for handling them. Is there some method that could be useful in handling negative emotions from the ego, in connection to the Will Process?

Releasing limiting emotions

Thank you for bringing this up - the activation of negative emotions is the dominant obstacle in all the steps in the Will Process, both in setting the goal, in deliberating it, in affirming it, in planning and in the execution of the plan.

Limiting beliefs, negative self-esteem, poor self-confidence are all based on emotions rather than on rational thought. Or more precisely, these obstacles are based on the emotional states with longer duration in time than for an "ordinary" emotion, states we call moods. An emotion caused by something happening has a typical duration of seconds or minutes. A mood can last hours, days, weeks, even months or years.

In a long-term emotional state or mood, negative emotions like worry, pessimism, self-abasement and so on, are upheld over time with corresponding thought patterns.

In order to train yourself to have full access to your Will Process, you may need to train your ability to handle limiting emotions activated by the Will Process.

A somewhat meditative method I often offer my clients, is included in the e-course "Release the Emotion", http://psykosyntesforum.se/ courses_release.htm.

The method, which I call "The Release Questions", works by closing your eyes and asking yourself certain specific questions, again and again, until your inner peace has returned.

Here is the instruction:

> Pose the following seven questions to yourself, over and over. Listen inwards, accept the answer Yes or No, whichever comes up after each question.

> 1. **Could I accept that this emotion exists in me**, as the physiological reaction it is, with the thoughts it leads to, with how it reinforces negative aspects of my self-image?

> 2. **Could I**, just now, **just let it be**, just as it is?

> 3. **Could I**, just now, even welcome it, and let myself just **have it**, fully?

> 4. **What is there beneath this emotion?**
> Is it deep down about that
> - I want to get respect,
> - I want to have control and/or
> - I want to feel secure?

> 5. **If this is so, could I let go of this ?**
> Could I release this emotion ?

6. **Would** I release this emotion ?

7. **When** could I do this ?

Repeat these seven "Release questions", again and again, fully focused each time.

Observe what maybe happens with the emotion.

Observe what maybe happens in your body, with your thoughts, with your self-image, with your presence, with your state of mind, just now.

If new negative emotions surface, release these as well with the same seven questions: accept, let it be, welcome it, what's under – acknowledgement, control or safety, could I let this go, would I let this go, when?

This method, which I have tested with positive and lasting results on hundreds of clients, is based on the theory that for all negative emotions the underlying cause is fear. Fear of not be accepted by others, fear of not having control of what will happen, fear of being harmed or punished.

The corresponding needs - acknowledgement, freedom and security - are natural and shared by us all. But if we instead of having these needs become driven by them, when we become compelled to get these needs met at any price, the outcome of our behavior may even become the opposite:

- The more we demand respect, the less we get.

- The more we try to control others, the less control we have.

- The more we try to create safety, the less secure we feel.

The e-course includes a chapter with the header "Set Goals Powerfully and Release Limiting Emotions", which describes a direct application of the Release Questions on setting up a goal and making an action plan.

Wonderful! The ego will be completely powerless!

I don't know if I can fully agree to that. But, I agree, with tools like these we can harness powers that are different and ultimately stronger than the ego's.

Yes - the ego expects a fight, expects resistance. Your methods are based on clarity of thought and complete acceptance of what is, and against this the ego is helpless.

Is this not what you said in ACOL:

> "This is all that is needed for the new to triumph over the old. There are no battles needed, no victories hard won through might and struggle. This is what is meant by surrender. We achieve victory now through surrender, an active and total acceptance of what is given."

Yes. There is no "right" or "wrong". The ego is not "wrong", it is just untrue. In your heart you will know when what you hear is true or not. What is not true isn't even worth to oppose. You can just observe it and let it go.

Again, you make it sound so simple. And in my experience it isn't...

I know it isn't, as long as your reality has you in its grip. This is why I have repeated the need of vigilance, vigilance for the Kingdom of God. But vigilance means not taking up a fight. Vigilance comes out of being present with what is, awareness, acceptance, inner peace and <u>will-power</u>: choose again.

When you said this, I suddenly got a clearer picture of why <u>all</u> the levels of consciousness, here described with the model of the chakras, are important in becoming an Elevated Self in Form. We are not through all the levels yet, but the picture I get so far is:

- Through **the Crown Chakra** I get Divine Inspiration.

- With my **Third Eye** I can envision my True Self, and can see my brothers and sisters with True Vision.

- Through my **Throat Chakra** I can communicate my Self clearly and honestly, and I can communicate the Mission I have taken on.

- Through my **Heart Chakra** I can extend the Love I am, and I can cultivate the energies of Love: acceptance, forgiveness, generosity, care, gratitude, compassion.

- With the help of an open **Solar Plexus** I can add Strong Will and Skilful Will to the Good Will of my Heart, and I can act with both inner power and inner peace.

	Name	Location	Element	Color	Qualities
	Crown	Top of the head	Information	Violet	Awareness, Knowledge
	Third Eye	Centre of forehead	Light	Indigo	Perception, Imagination
	Throat	Base of throat	Sound	Blue	Communication, Creativity
	Heart	Center of chest	Wind	Green	Compassion, Relationship
	Solar Plexus	Solar Plexus	Fire	Yellow	Will, Spontaneity, Self-esteem
	Sacral	Beneath the navel	Water	Orange	Feeling, Pleasure
	Base	Perineum	Earth	Red	Trust, Stability, Grounding

An excellent summing-up of this chapter. Shall we now continue downwards into even "denser" matter: your body's feelings, into the realm of pain and pleasure?

Yes, let's do that. Next chapter is about the Sacral Chakra, which is the second from the bottom.

When you mention pain and pleasure, I immediately get intrigued - you have said so much about our addiction to pain and the temptation of pleasure, both in ACIM and in ACOL. I am curious and I really looking forward to this next stage of our exploration!

6. The Sacral Chakra.

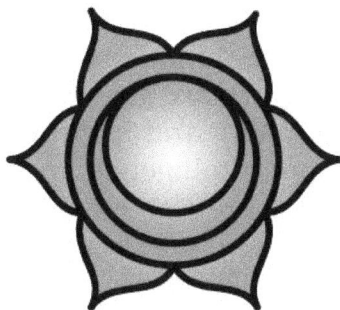

The Sacral Chakra is associated with the element of
water and is related to **emotion**, **need**, **desire**,
sensation, **pleasure**, **sexuality** and **passion**.

All these qualities are those that <u>motivate</u> us.
"Motivation", at its root, means "to move". Motivation
is what moves you into action, by motiv*ating* you can
move others into action.

When one is moved internally, one becomes inspired
to move externally in the world. We enjoy being
moved, whether it's by music, a touching poem, a
grand story, a passionate speech, a great love, a
fantastic vision.

The Sacral Chakra balances the fire in Solar Plexus -
although water can put out fire, fire can heat water to
make steam that can be used to run things. The fire
of your will can lead to burn-out if it's not tempered
with the waters of pleasure. If you work all the time
and never play, your work will suffer.

Balance

The element water stands for harmony, balance, relationship. The degree of openness of the Sacral Chakra can be balanced, too open or too closed.

Balanced: The positive qualities emanating from a balanced Sacral Chakra are graceful movement through life, spontaneity and playfulness, openness to change, emotional intelligence, nurturing abilities, healthy boundaries, ability to enjoy pleasure, sexual and sensual satisfaction, creativity, constructive passion.

Unbalanced: As the Sacral Chakra is closely connected to the body and the pleasures of the body, an indiscriminately wide open Sacral Chakra can lead to negative traits like drug or sexual addiction, obsessive attachments, mood swings, emotionality, over-sensitivity, poor boundaries, emotional dependency, instability.

Closed: A Sacral Chakra containing obstacles against the flow of life can lead to rigidity in your body, in beliefs or in behavior. It can cause insensitivity, fear of change, lack of desire and passion, avoidance of pleasure, fear of sexuality, poor social skills, closed boundaries, boredom.

The Law of Attraction

Within the New Age movement, the Sacral Chakra has been said to be connected to the Law of Attraction. The expression and interpretation of the Law of Attraction seems although sometimes have been influenced by ego thought patterns.

What has been seen as Attractiveness, where many proponents of the Law of Attraction believe that one's state of mind will attract what one wishes to have more of in one's life, is in reality <u>Creativity</u>.

An open and receptive Sacral Chakra will inspire your Inner Child, your playfulness and fantasy, and by this your creative abilities. You will, consciously and/or sub-consciously, <u>create</u> the life you want to have!

The joys of the body

Having come this far in my description of the Sacral Chakra, reading what I have written, I can sense that here, in connection with this level, there are many temptations of the body and of the physical world, temptations that can lead us away from our Path.

Posing the question to myself, "What shall I do to handle these temptations?", I can already hear you say "Just give all this over to The Holy Spirit". I am sorry my fantasy drags me ahead like this, but I can't help it - your anticipated answer makes me angry!

Firstly, be glad your fantasy works. Else this book would not have existed, and you would not have ventured into this exploration.

Your fantasy in this case led you astray - you know I never underestimate the obstacles in your world, and I would never say "Just do this". But this notwithstanding, your anger is important. Beneath the anger, what is there?

Hm. Frustration, I guess. This is a level of my own being I need to work with. In many respects I think my Sacral Chakra is rather closed, or at least there are many obstacles.

Good. Emotions are signals of needs, real or imagined. I think you would benefit from investigating which real needs you are not meeting.

*To broaden this dialogue, I think there is a need for large parts of humanity to seriously make this investigation - the western way of living has put an unbalanced emphasis on "*wants*", which really are cravings, and many have forgotten or lost contact with their true* needs.

For many, there is of course still a strong focus on the needs for survival, and they have not as yet the possibility to enjoy the luxury of thinking about what they want, or what they need more in life than mere survival.

But, an ever increasing number of people have passed this stage, and the state of the world, with social unrest, wars and an impending collapse of nature and climate, makes this investigation crucial.

What has to be investigated are the needs of the body versus the need of the soul. To become An Elevated Self in Form, you need to meet your spiritual needs and *you need to meet your body's needs. But for the body, these needs may have to be met in a new way, or with a new attitude, lest you fall prey to the temptations of the ego.*

True needs vs wants

The Holy Spirit will *handle this, but you have to become receptive first. The result of meeting one's true needs is not only Inner Peace, it is also* **Joy**.

The joy of following an inner calling. The joy of experiencing the flow, intensely and actively steering your boat, but <u>with</u> the stream. The joy of having your old self become Elevated, becoming your True Self but in form, here on Earth.

The crucial question you need to ask yourself is: "Which needs do I have to fulfil in order to experience this joy?"

Which needs have to be met for you to

- *Move gracefully through life.*
- *Experience spontaneity and playfulness.*
- *Become open to change.*
- *Develop your emotional intelligence.*
- *Develop your nurturing abilities.*
- *Have healthy boundaries.*
- *Be able to enjoy sexual and sensual pleasure.*
- *Be creative.*
- *Feel a glow inside for what you do.*
- *Become An Elevated Self in Form.*

An exercise, or a structure, that can be helpful in this investigation, is reminiscent of the exercise I described in the foreword of this book, Structured Meditation.

On a sheet of paper, make two columns, one named "What I truly need", the other "What I want".

Enter the period of time I called "<u>The Emptying Phase</u>". Fill in the two columns with your thoughts and ideas about your true needs versus your wants. Continue with this phase until the whole issue feels completely exhausted, and you cannot any longer come up with anything more at all, even if you try to force yourself to do it. Use as many sheets of paper as you need.

Secondly, *"The Reduction Phase"*:
Cut away the rightmost columns from your sheets of paper, and throw them away. Spend time, which again can be days or weeks, crossing out with a pencil any need that intuitively feels <u>less</u> important than the others, even if it may feel important in itself. Continue doing this until you have <u>ten</u> needs left on your list. Towards the end of this phase this may feel difficult, so take your time in selecting which ones to cross out. Be aware of the "demon" of the Sacral Chakra - guilt - which may tempt you to scratch out a need that might be central for you.

Thirdly and finally, the *"Receiving Phase"*:
Write down the ten True Needs left on your long list on a new sheet of paper, with large letters. Use colored pencils if you want to make them stand out clearer. Spend time each day, somewhere between half an hour to several hours, meditating on this list, or asking The Holy Spirit about them. Try to listen to your Inner Silence. Continue doing this for days or weeks.

If some of the True Needs on your list stills evokes other emotions than anticipation and joy, you may need to use the Belief Buster Lars described before, changing the image of yourself believing "Life is serious" into one where you truly believe and live the belief "Life is joy". Allowing yourself to be playful, even in a child-like way, will help you to open up to your creativity.

Another obstacle, one which I warned about in the description of the Reduction Phase above, is guilt or feelings of unworthiness, where you may feel that you have no right to demand that your needs be met. You need to remind yourself about one of the central Laws of God: giving and receiving are one. Or in this case, *receiving and giving are one. Also, when you stop judging your own needs, you will stop judging others'.*

This last obstacle is one I recognize as one stemming from conditioning. In the culture I have grown up in, and I suspect this may be the case in other cultures as well, being "needy" is seen as a negative trait.

I often give my clients the affirmation you mentioned before, as a home assignment to repeat to themselves many times each day:

> "My <u>and</u> others' needs are important.
> I can meet others' needs <u>better</u>,
> if I <u>also</u> meet my own."

I believe that blindly following the needs of one's ego can lead us astray, but by affirming the above we can become what can be called "Selfish in a sound way".

Giving and receiving are one

When you talked about giving and receiving being one, and here turned the original sentence around, I remembered an exercise we had in my training to become a therapist. In this exercise the group was subdivided into pairs. In the first half part of the exercise, half of us got the role of Receiver, the other half got the role Giver. After half the time, which was two hours in total, we switched roles.

In the room there were tables full of different things with which one could use for creating pleasure: massage tools and ointments, perfumes, fruit, small bowls with delicatessen, soft drinks, musical instruments, poetry books, and many other things.

The instruction for the Receiver was to describe a need that could be met with the things available, like a thorough foot massage, listening to the reading of poems of a specific poet, eating something specific, etc.

The instruction for the Giver was to, with the help of his or her knowledge and skills and with the help of the things that could be used, create an experience of pleasure for the Receiver.

At any time during the period of experiencing what the Giver offered, the Receiver was free to ask for something else, of for having something done differently.

I found this whole exercise to be extremely liberating, in two ways: in the role of Receiver, I could really allow myself to fully enjoy what my partner in the exercise had put together with the sole intent of giving me pleasure. As there was no expectation of me as the Receiver to give anything in return during this "receiving phase", I could really go into the experience, and there was no guilt, shame, embarrassment or any other negative emotion. I could also afterwards express my heartfelt gratitude to my partner for her inventiveness and skills.

In the role of the Giver, I to my surprise discovered that giving like this, just listening to the needs someone expresses and then to be able to fulfil these, was extremely joyful! I felt generous, creative, playful. It was really fun!

Afterwards when sharing our experiences, everybody agreed on that this exercise gave us several important insights:

- It is possible to <u>train</u> the ability for being Soundly Selfish.

- Giving and Receiving <u>are</u> one.

- Gratitude is closely connected to <u>joy</u>.

I know you have advised some of the couples you have in relationship coaching to do exercises resembling the one you have described here, but not as elaborate, more as an attitude to develop. Maybe you should give them as a home assignment to do the full exercise, with as much inventiveness as they can muster?

Yes, you are upon something important here. What could be more important in a relationship that includes sexuality than opening up the Sacral Chakra?

I will surely follow your advice!

Do you mean both as a therapist and as a husband?

Now you make me embarrassed... what if my wife reads this?

Ask her to do that. Have fun!

Even more embarrassed, I have to ask you: what do <u>you</u> know of these things?

I know a lot, old man. The ones that selected the stories about me to include in the Bible did though not see fit to include these parts of my life on Earth, as they did not believe that it could fit together with the image of God's Son according to the prophecies.

What they did not know or understand was that A Holy Relationship may well include sexuality, as the strong symbol of Unity it can be. And this is the case even more if you allow yourself to be playful and creative and to take delight in it.

In ACOL, I speak of sex in many places, for example like this:

> *"While you may, for a while yet, not see that all that are not expressions of love are expressions of fear, I assure you this is the case. Thus any behavior, including sexual behavior, that is not of love, is of fear."*

> *"You have determined sex to be the ultimate fulfillment of love and called it 'making love'. If it were painful rather than pleasurable, if you did not lose yourself and experience completion, you would not desire it. Sex, experienced for this pleasure and completion, regardless of emotional attachment or non-attachment, still would produce the desired effect of creating desire for oneness if you truly saw and understood the body and its acts as representative of truth. You have thought the things you do represent your drives, but they simply represent what was given to help you remember and return to who you truly are."*

So again, whether what you do is meaningful depends on what you use it <u>for</u>: to meet your ego's demands or to meet your own and others' True Needs.

As an Elevated Self in Form, you can live your life as you have always done, but on a new "platform", letting the physical realm be of service to you in representing your True Self instead of representing the small separated self you thought you were before.

So, if it is OK for you, I conclude this chapter with the following two observations:

- *Opening up your Sacral Chakra is an important step towards Enlightenment.*

- *Enlightenment implies not only Revelation; it is also to "Lighten Up", to bring Joy to the world.*

Now finally, we have come to the base of the matter, the Root Chakra.

It is OK with me to end here, as I cannot think of anything more just now to add to this chapter.

In starting to think about the next one I just now, even more than before, experience a complete lack of ideas or knowledge. But, having travelled this journey of exploration together with you has given me a sense of trust. So, with a lack of anxiety as well, or rather with a sense of anticipation, I approach "the end station" - The Root Chakra.

What I have added below has nothing to do with this chapter; it is more of a "meta processing" of the writing of this book, but I would like to end this chapter by quoting you from ACOL:

> "17.7 Each day is an unknown you enter into, despite your every attempt to anticipate what it might hold. And yet, while it would seem you would grow quite used to this phenomenon, you do not. You still make your plans and rail against everything that interferes with them, even knowing in advance that your greatest efforts at organization are often to no avail. A Course in Miracles asks you to 'receive instead of plan', and yet few of you

understand the meaning of this simple instruction or what it says to you of the unknown.

17.8 What it says is that the unknown is benevolent. What it says is that what you cannot anticipate can be anticipated for you. What it says is that you could be receiving constant help if you would but let it come. What it says is that you are not alone.

17.9 Receiving implies that something is being given. Receiving implies a willingness to accept what is given."

7. The Root Chakra.

In the last step in our manifestation process towards becoming an Elevated Self in Form we now come down to the Root Chakra, to the element of **earth**, where we shall ground all our hard work into the material world, into the physical resting place of manifestation.

If you do everything else in this book but fail to ground your work in your earthly reality, the "Happy Dream" of bringing God's Love to Earth, of becoming an Elevated Self in form, will not hold solid.

This level of manifestation creates the greatest resistance of all the chakra steps, because you are now hitting solid ground. Resistance is the tendency of matter to prevent change, and it is a useful principle. If the earth had no resistance, you couldn't walk on it.

You have to bring the fire and the power of the Solar Plexus into play with the water of the Heart Chakra and the earth of the Root Chakra to make something that is of true service. But, this level is exacting and demanding. This may make you hesitate, but if you accept the demands and work with them, they will actually <u>support</u> your dream, all the way to completion.

The Sanskrit name of the Root Chakra, Muladhara, means "root support." The deeper the roots, the higher and bigger the plant can grow. The more grounded you are, the more easily you can manifest. Roots have both masculine and feminine qualities. On the masculine side, they penetrate the earth, pushing their way downward between rocks and soil. The feminine aspect of roots is receptive, drawing nourishment and moisture up from the earth to make the plant grow.

You can also liken your body to a high temple tower in which your chakras are the different floors. The Root Chakra is your foundation, which must be solid enough for the temple to hold the divine energies that come down from above. A common cause for psychological distress in a spiritual crisis is an underdeveloped Root Chakra.

As you bring heaven down to earth, each chakra's activities feed and inform the chakra below it. When you receive guidance and clarify your intention in the Crown Chakra, it is easier to create a clear vision in the Third Eye. When your vision is clear, it's easier to define your goals and communicate and convey your intentions through your Throat Chakra. Clear communication is also the foundation for good relationships, through your Heart Chakra. Enlivening your love nourishes you and others, generating the energy from which you derive your power and the motivation to do the things that need to be done through your Solar Plexus. With each successful step forward, you feel the spark of pleasure in your Sacral

Chakra, and you experience that creation is joy, so you keep going even when the going gets tough. Fun greases the gears for a smooth journey.

Each step is important. But if you are not fully committed to fulfilling each one, your dream cannot be birthed into physical reality. Committed in energy, heart, and mind. Commitment is an alignment of all your chakras, following through on all requirements of each level, down to committing your entire Self, with the help of you Root Chakra, to complete your Mission to the last detail.

I thought I was a preacher. Now I hear that you as well are inclined in that direction.

What, have I been too lengthy?

Maybe a little ;) I think our readers will have to read what you have written above at least twice, to get all you want to convey. But having said this, I think you should, dear reader. And when you have done so, I think you will understand and you will then probably regard Lars' text as a good description. I, for my part, see it as an excellent overview of the symbolic functions of the chakras. (Remember: symbolic - this is not "the truth". But the chakra system, as the rest of the body, if used properly, can serve you as a sign post, <u>pointing</u> at Truth.)

So, no offence, Lars. After your description here, I can really see why you chose the symbolism of the Chakra System as the foundation for this exploration.

But, explain more: more exactly, what is it one has to commit to?

A couple of things, I think.

Firstly, I think that I want to commit myself to listening to <u>my Inner Guidance</u>, trusting that I will be led.

Secondly, I want to clarify <u>my personal Mission</u> to myself, and when needed, to others, and to commit myself into really accomplishing this Mission.

Thirdly, I want my commitment to be "<u>whole-hearted</u>" as ACOL defines it. And, using the symbolism of this book here, I want to use all my chakra energies optimally in my commitment.

You sound wholehearted! But, we are now deep down into the realm of the physical and of concrete action. To commit like you describe it, what will you actually <u>do</u>?

Way back on my personal path, when my mind alone ruled, I was committed to what I had set up to do. But, as I did not listen to my inner guidance, even if I now know I already then got clear signals from my heart, I made "rational" plans - I analyzed possible gains and risks, and I put together action plans.

Looking back, I now realize how I struggled. It now feels as if I spent most of my energy as if I all the time tried to swim against a strong current.

Since then, I have learned from you to refrain from making plans as my first step, and instead just relax in trust, and let myself receive guidance. This did not happen suddenly, but after having read what you said about this in many places in ACIM a number of times, it gradually sunk in, and in what I do

nowadays, it more and more often feels like swimming
<u>with</u> a strong current.

In what I do nowadays, I pretty much follow your
advice in ACIM, specifically the concluding questions
in lesson 71:

> **"Only God's plan for salvation works.**
>
> (...) God's plan for salvation works simply because, by
> following His direction, you seek for salvation where it
> is. But if you are to succeed, as God promises you will,
> you must be willing to seek there only. Otherwise, your
> purpose is divided and you will attempt to follow two
> plans for salvation that are diametrically opposed in all
> ways. The result can only bring confusion, misery and a
> deep sense of failure and despair.
>
> How can you escape all this? Very simply. The idea for
> today is the answer. Only God's plan for salvation will
> work. There can be no real conflict about this, because
> there is no possible alternative to God's plan that will
> save you. His is the only plan that is certain in its
> outcome. His is the only plan that must succeed.
>
> Let us practice recognizing this certainty today. And let
> us rejoice that there is an answer to what seems to be a
> conflict with no resolution possible. All things are
> possible to God. Salvation must be yours because of His
> plan, which cannot fail.
>
> Begin the two longer practice periods for today by
> thinking about today's idea, and realizing that it
> contains two parts, each making equal contribution to
> the whole. God's plan for your salvation will work, and
> other plans will not. Do not allow yourself to become
> depressed or angry at the second part; it is inherent in
> the first. And in the first is your full release from all
> your own insane attempts and mad proposals to free

yourself. They have led to depression and anger; but God's plan will succeed. It will lead to release and joy.

Remembering this, let us devote the remainder of the extended practice periods to asking God to reveal His plan to us. Ask Him very specifically:

What would You have me do?
Where would You have me go?
What would You have me say, and to whom?"

Good! But, knowing you, knowing your keen mind, I also know you do not just ask these questions at every step you take.

No, I have to admit I don't. When I have to decide on a major goal on what to do, I seek inner guidance. But when I feel I have received it, which I sometimes experience as a thought "I haven't thought my self", or which I at other times more experience as a hunch, I set up a concrete goal and a specified action plan, to which I then commit.

SMART goals vs MAC goals.

In my profession I have often worked in the role of an organizational consultant. Common practice in this area of work has been to talk about "SMART" goals: specific, measurable, achievable, realistic and time-bound.

Nowadays, I regard this is as an obsolete idea, based in the ego's belief in a world of lack and separation. Specific may fool you that you know better than The Holy Spirit. Achievable and Realistic may limit you from being open for miracles. <u>Time-related</u> may make you think that what is worth doing always takes time - again closing yourself to the miracle. The miracle can have effects even in past time!

Instead, I have started to use a new concept:
MAC goals: <u>Measurable</u>, <u>Attractive</u> and <u>Commitment-based</u>.

The only thing kept from SMART goals is <u>measurable</u>, which I think is necessary. With measureable I of course mean that there has to be some physical criterion that you can measure, in order to know whether you are approaching your goal and to know when you have reached it. But I also mean that the goal shall be possible to <u>envision</u>, using your imagination to place yourself at the time of success and allowing yourself to really experience the concrete and measurable results, and to allow yourself to experience the satisfaction and joy to have reached your goal.

The second letter A in my acronym, <u>Attractive</u>: the goal, and the goal image, shall engender anticipation and enthusiasm, both in yourself and in others. It doesn't matter whether the goal is "realistic" or "achievable", those criteria are only expressions of your ego's beliefs in lack of possibility or limited resources. If you commit to a heart-felt goal, new possibilities will emerge, resources will appear. As the philosopher Platon (427-347 BC) said

> "By believing passionately in something that still does not exist, we create it. The nonexistent is whatever we have not sufficiently desired."

The third letter C, <u>Commitment-based</u> is closely connected to the Root Chakra. It is also connected to the Will Process, which I described in connection to Solar Plexus, and in this specifically each one of the steps <u>Decide</u>, <u>Affirm</u>, <u>Plan,</u> <u>Act</u> and <u>Evaluate</u>.

Commitment is furthermore not only about committing to pursue the goal you have set up, it shall also be a commitment for doing it with <u>attention</u> and <u>care</u>, with continued focus on the details and on quality. In building a car, if you forget some of the screws and bolts, you will soon have a car falling apart. With all of them in place, and firmly adjusted, you have a vehicle that will take you wherever you want to go.

For one who quite recently said, about starting on this chapter "In starting to think about the next one I just now, even more than before, experience a complete lack of ideas or knowledge", there seems to be some discrepancy between your self-image and what you do...

Ha! I am starting to see through you. You know as well as I do now, how inspiration works, how it is to "be in the flow". But... and I just realized this ... you are testing me! Checking to see whether my ego could be triggered into counter-attacking the seeming criticism.

Or, testing you to see whether you can see through me. Test accomplished successfully. I am happy that you no longer regard me as a keeper of secrets. But, forgive me for the interruption - continue! What is more important, in opening up one's Root Chakra?

The Now Rules

Ah, well, no - I don't need to forgive you. Rather, I thank you for interrupting and by this again reminding me of my tendency to preach...

But OK. Next what is important around concrete action are what I call The Now Rules. Through my company I offer an e-course in personal efficiency, where the central message is that most people work hard and efficiently, but that many waste energy unnecessarily by poor planning, allowing themselves to be interrupted and by postponing things.

(The course is called ETT, Eliminate the Time Thieves, http://psykosyntesforum.se/courses_ett.htm.)

The Now Rules are:

- DO IT <u>NOW</u>. (Cardinal rule.)

- DO IT <u>CORRECTLY</u> NOW.
  (Re-doing things is a waste of time.)

- <u>FORMULATE</u> IT CLEARLY NOW.
  (Misunderstandings cost a lot of time.)

- <u>DECIDE</u> NOW.
  (Delaying decisions steals time from many.)

- SOLVE <u>PROBLEMS</u> NOW, while they are small.
  (Typical increase: a factor 2 per day...)

- It takes less time doing it right than explaining why you did it incorrectly ...

When The Now Rules are not applicable, due to external factors you cannot control, <u>then</u> you <u>plan</u>.

In the ETT course, I recommend having an efficient planning tool, and to have only one. More than one, like different calendars, lists on the side, reminder post-its, etc, leads also into wasting energy. If your planning tool is computer-based, it should be set up such that you will be reminded when the task is due. In this way, your planning tool will help you to "<u>remember to forget</u>". This is important - many suffering from burn-out have ended up there by trying to keep hundreds of different things in their minds all the time. The human brain is actually capable to hold only seven things (plus/minus two) in awareness simultaneously.

Good concrete and grounding advice. But what you have been talking about up to now has mostly been around the mind and how to use methods that serve your mind in a good way. This is good and very useful, but what about the body itself?

God created the individual Self as means to know Himself in a new and deeper way, through Relationship in Unity. The individual Self then chose to express Itself in physical form, thereby creating the physical world. This was done out of Love, and was wholly consistent with God's Laws and with Creation.

What then happened was that the individual Self got preoccupied with Its individuality, and forgot that It existed in Unity. It got the little mad idea that it could be a personal self, self-sufficient. This "mad idea" evoked fear and the advent of the erroneous image of God as angry and vengeful, and reinforced the amnesia with guilt.

You are the same as you were before expressing yourself in physical form, and the physical world and your bodies are not "wrong" or illusionary in themselves. They are merely a result of a choice. The illusionary is the belief in separation and specialness, as this has made you see only the physical, and made you either believe that the physical realm is all there is, or to believe in a dualistic existence, where "Heaven" is somewhere else. Remember that I said already two thousand years ago: "Heaven is within you."

So, in remembering this, the first step is to express your True Self through your body, with its mind, thoughts and emotions. This is what I have called the Elevated Self in Form, and this is what this whole exploration has been about.

Now, having come down to the symbol of the Root Chakra, we can let it serve us as a tool for Elevating form itself. As you said above, the body can be likened to a temple, and the Root Chakra can be likened to the foundation, which needs to be solid and stable.

You are right - I tend to focus on the mind, and by this I often forget what a useful and necessary tool the body is in spiritual growth.

Here are a couple of body exercises I have used in my coaching and therapeutic work:

Inhabit and ground your body

Stand on the floor with bare feet, shoulder width apart. Turn your feet slightly inwards and bend your knees so they are just above your toes, such that when looking down, you see your big toes inside of your kneecaps. Push firmly into both feet, as if you were trying to push the floorboards apart. Feel how your feet and legs grip the ground and feel the power in your pelvic area, how your whole body feels more solid.

Now, charge the Root Chakra by inhaling slowly and deeply through your nose, bending down deeper as you do this. Them, exhale slowly through your mouth, as if you were blowing out a candle, as you slowly straighten your legs. Let them straighten to a position where your knees are still somewhat bent (locking the knees will shut off the charge you are building).

Repeat this downward and upward movement several times, inhaling through your nose as you sink down, slowly surrendering to gravity, and exhaling through your mouth as you slowly straighten up, forcefully "pushing the earth down".

You may start to feel a subtle trembling in your legs, which is a sign of that you are doing the exercise correctly. The life energy "chi" is increasing in your body. Continue until your legs are really shaking.

Doing this exercise on a regular basis will help you ground yourself over time, as it employs both the masculine and the feminine aspects of rootedness - finding your inner stability by pushing into the ground, nourishing yourself by pulling earth energy up through your body and into your chakras. Any remaining blocks you may have in any of your chakras will dissolve with this exercise.

Find you inner balance

In this second exercise, you need a partner. The exercise will utilize the first position described in the exercise above, which I here will call the Grounded Position.

But first, in order to experience contrast, position yourself differently: stand straight with your feet tightly together and with your knees firmly locked, feeling how you almost press them backwards. Close your eyes.

In this position, your partner shall without warning press sideways on your shoulders, or shall push you backwards by pressing on your chest, or push you forwards by pressing on your back. Your partner shall mix directions in a random way.

Feel how you each time you are pushed lose your balance, and how you have to take a step in some direction in order to not fall. Feel how your partner needs only quite weak force to topple you over. Feel how your growing insecurity will make you breathe high up in your chest. Notice which emotions this part of the exercise evoke, probably increasing stress and insecurity

Now, open your eyes and go into the Grounded Position. Let you breathing calm down, until you can feel how you breathe deep down, using your diaphragm, and your pulse slows down.

With a nod, let your partner start to push you again, in the same way as before. Feel how being bodily grounded, and really present to what is happening through both seeing and hearing, makes you able to keep your balance, whatever your partner does. Let your partner experiment with increasing force, and see how much more forcefully he or she has to push you before you have to move a foot in order to regain your balance. Feel how gracefully and efficiently you now can counteract the forces acting on your body.

Feel how your breathing and your pulse stay low and steady. Notice your emotions - they probably convey strength, security, inner stability, pride of yourself!

Imagine symbolically being in this state of mind in all different situations of your life, even without having to position your body like this. Imagine how you can come into this state by just remembering this exercise, by just visualizing how it feels to stand steadily and grounded like this.

Good exercises! Being an Elevated Self in Form is not only about letting your mind be in Unity, to be Christ-minded. Your body needs to be fully aligned with this: it needs to be fully grounded in Form, thereby making Form into what it was originally meant to be - an expression of the Divine.

It feels like we together are approaching the end of this exploration. In our previous one, in the book "Jesus on Catching the Bull", we explored the "journey up to the mountain top". In this book, we have explored the journey back down to earth again, and now it feels like we have "closed the circle". I have nothing more I want to add.

It would though be a nice contrast to my "preachings" if you could end this chapter, maybe with some concluding thoughts around the chakra system.

Yes, we are approaching the end of this particular exploration and of this book. With your underlining of the word "this" above, I guess you are implying that we will pursue more explorations together in the future. We surely will, and I am looking forward to it!

And yes, I will end this chapter, but not with concluding thoughts, as I think you have explained things well, covering many aspects of the journey towards becoming An Elevated Self in Form. I will conclude with a visualization.

In this visualization, I will use a concept you have often used, Logical Levels from Bateson's systems theory:

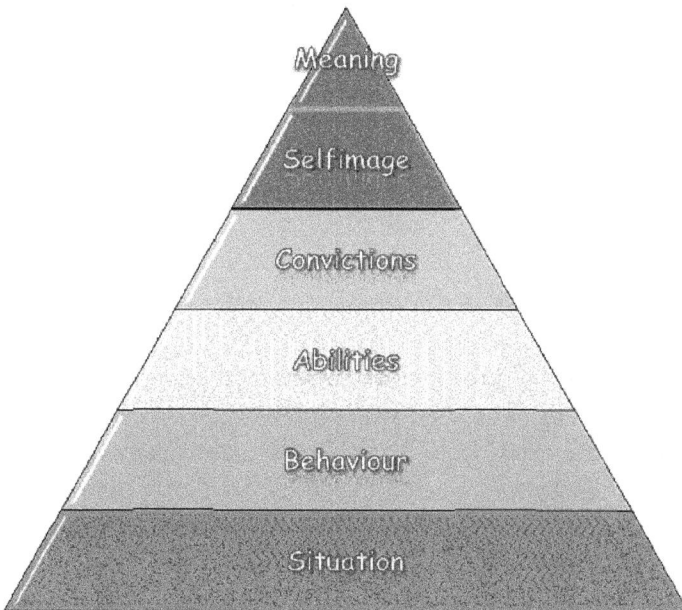

A visualization directly from Jesus - that's new!

Not that new, I offered one before when we talked about the Heart Chakra, and also, my telling of parables two thousand years ago worked at that time in a similar way. And in my teachings to the disciples I often made them use their imagination to envision themselves finding their Unity with our Father.

Visualizations may feel difficult to use in written form. Would it be OK if I recorded myself reading your visualization, so that our readers can go into it with their eyes closed?

That's a very good idea. Where can they find it?

They can listen to it streaming or they can download it at

http://psykosyntesforum.se/
PsF_0897_Jesus_on_Elevated_Form/
Chakra_Grounding.mp3

Chakra Grounding

Sit comfortably and close your eyes.

Imagine a time when you have come very far on your Path towards becoming an Elevated Self in Form. This time may be now, or it may for you still be in the future. Imagine seeing yourself from a short distance, how you can see how the you over there really represents a True Self, in expression, in body posture, in what radiates out.

Imagine now going into this image of yourself, experiencing how it is, with thoughts, emotions, how your body feels.

You know that you have worked with yourself for a long time, and you have now finally opened yourself completely into being United with God, through Christ Consciousness. You have since long learnt that the meaning of your life is to be a messenger of Truth, but you also know that you will convey this message to your brothers and sisters in your individual, unique way. A way that may be in words, or through deeds, or it may be conveyed through just being who you are in Truth.

Experience now how God's Truth enters you from above, streaming into you through your Crown Chakra, like a Divine Golden Light. A long time ago, you became aware of this entrance point for Divine Energy to flow into your body, and you have worked diligently to open it completely. Feel how the warm, Golden Light enters your body, how it flows into your mind, into your thoughts and emotions, into every cell of your body. Feel how this has made you truly open-minded, in complete and direct Unity with God.

Experience how this Light makes it possible for you to see truly, even with your physical eyes closed. Imagine seeing yourself out in the world as An Elevated Self in Form, see how you convey the message of Truth to others, and how this influences them. Experience how your work in opening up the chakra of The Third Eye has made you able to envision your future in vivid detail. How this vision has made you look at yourself in a new way, as a person completely free of the ego. And how this has made you able to see lovingly upon each and every of your brothers and sisters, with complete tolerance and forgiveness.

Feel how the warm light of God's Truth flows down and enlivens your Throat Chakra. Sense how your work in opening up this channel has made it possible for you to convey your personal Mission, even if it is just to yourself. Sense how in doing this, you feel how your beliefs in yourself have become strong and liberating. Imagine conveying your Mission to others in words, or by deeds, or through just being your True Self. Experience how, when you do this, it influences them, how they hear and respect your honesty and your sincerity.

And, now, feel how the warm Golden Light fills your heart, and how it flows out into the world through your wide-open Heart Chakra, how you extend your gentleness, your generosity and your love. Imagine how you do this in many different ways, in your words, in what you do, and in just being your True Self. Experience how, when you do this, you can really feel how giving and receiving are one. The more love you give, the more you receive. The more generous you are, the more you experience abundance. The gentler you are, the more benevolent Universe will appear. And feel how your Heart Energy radiates through your whole body, your mind and your emotions, how it makes you whole-hearted in everything you do.

The Golden Light of God's Love transforms to pure energy when it flows through your Solar Plexus, and it makes you act in the world in a whole-hearted and focused way. Imagine how you now always act with awareness and purposefulness, and how this really makes an impact on the world. Feel how this inner power strengthens your faith in yourself and in God.

Feel how this strengthens your courage, and how you never need to defend yourself or to defend what you believe. In everything you do, you are faithful to and vigilant for God's Kingdom and your Holy Mission, awakening your brothers and sisters to their True Selves.

As you feel how the Golden Light of God's Truth flows further downwards in your body and passes through your Sacral Chakra, you can now experience the joy of being able to act purposefully, feeling how the joy fuels your willpower even more. The joy of accomplishing what you have set up to do. The joy from seeing the positive results of your actions, of extending God's Love into the world. The joy of being called to a Holy Mission and of receiving God's Grace in following it, under His guidance. And when things do not happen according to your old personal self's expectations, how your joy helps you to be patient, trusting God to lead you. Feel how your whole body, as the Divine Temple it is, in itself is a joyful celebration of you as The Elevated Self in Form you are.

And finally, feel how the Golden Light reaches your Root Chakra, and how with this, it has filled your whole body, all your thoughts, all your emotions, with the warm and embracing Love of God. Experience fully with your inner vision how the Golden Light of God's Truth and God's Love shines out from you, encloses you in a sphere of Golden Light. See how this sphere of Light expands more and more. Upwards, increasingly uniting with God. Outwards, uniting with your brothers and sisters in the world. Downwards, into the ground, and how the flow of Life goes both downwards into Earth, and upwards from the Earth. Feel how this energy of Life now flows freely through your whole body, through your mind, through your emotions, both upwards and downwards at the same time.

Experience how the upward flow liberates you completely from the old personal self you were before, and experience how the downward flow makes you manifest your new Self, an Elevated Self in Form, out into the world. And feel how you now are accomplished, how you can relax in complete Trust. Trust in being both connected in Unity with the Divine and being grounded firmly in the physical realm, in your body, in your actions, in your relationships with your brothers and sisters.

And with this, my beloved, I say: So Be It - Amen.

Epilogue.

What a wonderful visualization...

For me, it reminded me of an image Roberto Assagioli (founder of Psychosynthesis) described, when talking about the "Peak Experience". This is an experience many have had, and I have had it a few times in my life. It is an experience of Revelation, of feeling One with All, but it is often comes only as a short glimpse. Most people that have had an experience like this find it difficult to describe it in words.

Assagioli said that these types of experiences were invaluable and to be treasured and remembered, but that they could be likened to a "helicopter trip to the peak of the mountain". Being there, one can experience the full beauty and the serenity, but only from a distance as it is not possible to land on the peak. In order to reach the peak and to stand on it yourself, you have to fly back down to ground level again, and then you have to embark on your journey up to the peak, by climbing yourself. Each person has to find his or her own path up there.

Still, having seen this glimpse is what motivates me to climb...

What motivates your _mind_, yes. Your _Heart_ has always known.

Your reminder touches something inside of me, making be believe you completely. Thank you, Jesus.

And thank you for having been my "travelling partner" on this part of my Path towards the Peak! I am not up there yet by far, but it feels like I have climbed a good way up.

But one thing still disturbs me. This image of the mountain - it conveys <u>one</u> reality. Ground level seems to symbolize our every-day experience in our physical world. But the <u>whole</u> mountain is real, as real at its base as at the peak.

Despite this, I have met many ACIM students that describe "ground level" as imaginary, as an illusion. Even the editor of ACIM, Kenneth Wapnick, was a very strong proponent of this description.

But here we have been describing The Elevated Self in Form, and I cannot read into your descriptions of this as it being illusionary. On the contrary, you say that being An Elevated Self in Form is meeting the conditions for being able to experience "The Happy Dream".

Misinterpretations are common and unavoidable. Many of these are naturally a result of ego resistance, which should come as no surprise.

The interpretation that dear Kenneth was such a proponent for, which I agree he was, was though not at all ego-driven. It was a result of his need of standing firm against strong forces that arose around him when ACIM was first published. Unwittingly, he ended up in the position that the physical reality as you perceive it was an illusion in itself, and that God's Kingdom was the only True Reality. I say unwittingly, because despite the fact that Kenneth firmly believed in non-dualism, his interpretation actually reflected a dualistic view.

My message in ACIM was, and is, that existence of the ALL is non-dualistic. At each and every place in ACIM I talk about illusion, I talk about "the illusion of the ego".

With this I mean that it is the <u>belief</u> that is illusionary, and I have described in many places in ACIM how this belief made you "blind", even "unconscious", unable to see how the physical realm is but a part of, an <u>aspect</u> of Reality. What you see, in this limited state of mind that makes you believe that only what you see is real and the only reality there is, can be called illusion. Your state of mind will also make you "see" things that <u>are</u> illusionary, like sin, and separation.

As ACIM sometimes became interpreted with a dualistic stance, albeit people talked much about non-dualism, I recognized the need for correcting this misinterpretation. And this was <u>one</u> of the reasons I asked Mari Perron to scribe A Course of Love. There were many other reasons, but correcting common misinterpretations of ACIM was one.

I am relieved to hear you say this. In order to not having to repeat things you have already said in ACOL, are there any particular passages in ACOL that you think are useful in understanding non-dualism and the seeming contradiction between the physical and the Divine?

There are many, but let me first show you some passages from ACIM which illustrate what I said above about the ego's illusions:

> *T-4.III.1. "It is hard to understand what 'The Kingdom of Heaven is within you' really means. This is because it is not understandable to the ego, which interprets it as if something outside is inside, and this does not mean anything. The word 'within' is unnecessary. The Kingdom of Heaven <u>is</u> you. What else <u>but</u> you did the Creator create, and what else but you is His Kingdom? This is the whole message of the Atonement; a message which in its totality transcends the sum of its parts. You,*

too, have a Kingdom that your spirit created. It has not ceased to create because of the ego's illusions. Your creations are no more fatherless than you are. Your ego and your spirit will never be co-creators, but your spirit and your Creator will always be. Be confident that your creations are as safe as you are.

<u>The Kingdom is perfectly united and perfectly protected, and the ego will not prevail against it. Amen.</u>"

T-4.V.4. "The body is the ego's home by its own election. It is the only identification with which the ego feels safe, since the body's vulnerability is its own best argument that you cannot be of God. This is the belief that the ego sponsors eagerly. Yet the ego hates the body, because it cannot accept it as good enough to be its home. Here is where the mind becomes actually dazed. Being told by the ego that it is really part of the body and that the body is its protector, the mind is also told that the body cannot protect it. Therefore, the mind asks, 'Where can I go for protection?' to which the ego replies, 'Turn to me.' The mind, and not without cause, reminds the ego that it has itself insisted that it is identified with the body, so there is no point in turning to <u>it</u> for protection. The ego has no real answer to this because there is none, but it does have a typical solution. It obliterates the question from the mind's awareness. Once out of awareness the question can and does produce uneasiness, but it cannot be answered because it cannot be asked."

C-4.1. "The world you <u>see</u> is an illusion of a world."

C-4.2. "The body's eyes are therefore not the means by which the real world can be seen."

When you said before how you in ACIM talk about the <u>ego's</u> illusions "at each and every place in ACIM", I used my electronic copy of ACIM and scanned all three books of ACIM for the word "illusion". The Textbook contains 458 instances, the Workbook 230, the Manual 70, Clarification of Terms 25, and the rest 46, all in all 829 instances. I have studied each of these instances, and I can understand your point, even if I have to say that some of the instances were not as clear as others with respect to clarifying your definition of the word "illusion", as being what comes out of the ego's power over us, making us "blind" to God's Reality.

I really love you Inner Engineer, Lars, describing spiritual matters in mathematical terms! But I understand your need of consistency and logic. I have to admit that some of the parts where I talked about illusion may not have been crystal clear, but it is important to remember the context in which ACIM was introduced, and that the primary purpose of ACIM was to challenge the collective ego's claims of owning the Truth about Reality.

ACIM was aimed at influencing the mind, by breaking down the multitude of erroneous and limiting beliefs imposed by the ego.

Thirty years later, the world had changed, partly thanks to the message of ACIM and similar messages that have come through to mankind by other channels.

In this new context, ACOL came, in a small part to clarify some of the things in ACIM that had become misinterpreted or not fully understood, but mostly as a necessary sequel to ACIM. Where ACIM spoke to your minds, the purpose of ACOL was to speak to your Hearts.

I can subscribe to that - reading ACOL was a much more emotional experience for me than reading ACIM ever was. If you allow my persistent Engineer to continue, ACOL has only 100 instances of the word "illusion". Does this illustrate anything about what we are talking about?

It does, even if I have not purposefully limited the number of times I used the word "illusion". But still, even if the ultimate aim of ACOL is the same as that of ACIM, to teach how to remove all obstacles against realizing who you are in Truth, there is in ACOL more focus on how to achieve The Happy Dream, how to Elevate your personal self into becoming An Elevated Self still remaining in the illusion of being only in form. Note: form is not illusionary in itself, but the <u>belief</u> that form is all there is, is illusionary.

I have described this in many places in ACOL, for example like this:

> ACOL
> "19.1 There was no evil intent in the creation of the body as a learning device, and as a learning device it was perfectly created. The problem lies in what you have, in your forgetfulness, made of the body. Only from thinking of the body as yourself did ideas of glorifying the body arise. To glorify a learning device makes no sense. And yet in creating the perfect device from which you could experience separation, all such problems were anticipated and corrective devices created alongside them. You could not fully experience separation without a sense of self as separate, and you could not fully experience anything without your free will. A separate self with a free will operating in an external world, as well as a spirit self desiring the experience of separation, would naturally lead to a situation where the whole range of experiences available to a separate being would exist."

The third Treatise
"12.8. Let's return a moment to the choice that was made for the human experience, the choice to express whom you are in the realm of physicality. You were not "better" or more "right" before this choice was made than you are now. You made a choice consistent with the laws of creation and the steps of creation outlined above. From this choice, many experiences ensued. Some of these experiences were the result of fear, some the result of love. The choice to express who you are in physical terms was not a choice made of fear but made of love. A physical self is not inconsistent with the laws of God or of creation. It is simply a choice.

12.9 The life of the physical self became a life of suffering and strife only because the physical or personal self forgot that it exists in relationship and believed itself to be separate and alone. In its fear, it made an ego-self which, because it sprang from fear, was not consistent with the laws of Love or of creation. Knowing it existed in a state inconsistent with that of the laws of God, it made of God a being to be feared, thus continuing, and being unable to find release from, the cycle of fear.

12.10 What would be a greater step in all of creation than a physical self able to choose to express the Self within the laws of love? A physical self, able to express itself from within the House of Truth in ways consistent with peace and love is the next step in creation, the rebirth of the Son of God known as the resurrection.

12.11 While this would seem to say that mistakes may occur within creation, remember that creation is about change and growth. There is no right or wrong within creation but there are stages of growth and change. Humankind is now passing through a tremendous stage of growth and change. Are you ready?"

Wonderful passages. Reading them reminds me of the feeling of relief I felt when I first read them, and when I read other similar passages in ACOL. The relief of not having to deny anything in my present reality.

The only thing I need to do (which is not so "only"...) is to keep expanding my sense of what is real to me.

On your question "Are you ready?", my answer just now is "no", or possibly "maybe". But <u>this</u> I can say with conviction - I am willing! Isn't this what you said would be enough?

Yes and no. At the stage you were at when taking the course as presented in ACIM, it was enough. But now, if you want to be a serious student of ACOL, I have called you to have more than "just a little willingness":

> *The second Treatise*
> *"11.9 This learning, then, must be seen for what it is. It is the holiest of work and the final evidence of means and end being the same. Your devotion to this learning must now be complete, <u>your willingness total</u>, your way of learning that of a mind and heart joined in wholeheartedness."*

This is what I expect of you, this is what I call you to do, if you really want to become An Elevated Self in Form.

I fully accept that, as I feel deep down that this "demand" is not a demand from you, it comes as a wish and a longing - it is a calling in full strength from my own Heart!

I now I feel that this exploration has come to its end for me, and that I have come to the end of this book. Somehow I know within myself that the last thing you said above is the last thing you wish to say in this book.

So, on a personal note, the last thing I wish to say is Thank you, Jesus. Thank you for the profound learning the writing of this book has been to me. Thank you for everything.

I was on the verge of thanking you for taking your time, when I realized that you haven't, being outside of it...

It is my sincere hope, dear reader, that you have learned something from reading this book, and that it will become useful to you on your own individual Path towards Truth and to God.

God bless you.

With love

Lars G

Lars Gimstedt

Linköping, Sweden, June 1 2015.

www.ingramcontent.com/pod-product-compliance
Lightning Source LLC
Chambersburg PA
CBHW060758050426
42449CB00008B/1440